PREPPER

What You Will Need to Be Prepared for an Emergency and Natural Disaster or Apocalypse

(A Beginners Prepping Guide to Survive a Disaster in the Wilderness)

Charles Fisher

Published by Oliver Leish

Charles Fisher

All Rights Reserved

Prepper: What You Will Need to Be Prepared for an Emergency and Natural Disaster or Apocalypse (A Beginners Prepping Guide to Survive a Disaster in the Wilderness)

ISBN 978-1-77485-112-8

All rights reserved. No part of this guide may be reproduced in any form without permission in writing from the publisher except in the case of brief quotations embodied in critical articles or reviews.

Legal & Disclaimer

The information contained in this book is not designed to replace or take the place of any form of medicine or professional medical advice. The information in this book has been provided for educational and entertainment purposes only.

The information contained in this book has been compiled from sources deemed reliable, and it is accurate to the best of the Author's knowledge; however, the Author cannot guarantee its accuracy and validity and cannot be held liable for any errors or omissions. Changes are periodically made to this book. You must consult your doctor or get professional medical advice before using any of the suggested remedies, techniques, or information in this book.

Upon using the information contained in this book, you agree to hold harmless the Author from and against any damages, costs, and expenses, including any legal fees potentially resulting from the application of any of the information provided by this guide. This disclaimer applies to any damages or injury caused by the use and application, whether directly or indirectly, of any advice or information presented, whether for breach of contract, tort, negligence, personal injury, criminal intent, or under any other cause of action.

You agree to accept all risks of using the information presented inside this book. You need to consult a professional medical practitioner in order to ensure you are both able and healthy enough to participate in this program.

Table of Contents

CHAPTER 1: DEFINITIONS 1

CHAPTER 2: THE PURPOSE OF A BUGOUT BAG 11

CHAPTER 3: SOURCING YOUR ITEMS CHEAPLY 16

CHAPTER 4: WATER STORAGE 23

CHAPTER 5: HOW IMPORTANT IS IT TO BE PHYSICALLY PREPARED FOR A DISASTER? 27

CHAPTER 6: PRESERVING FRESH FOODS 30

CHAPTER 7: FOOD 37

CHAPTER 8: ESSENTIAL PREPPER'S MEDICAL/SANITATION SUPPLIES 43

CHAPTER 9: FOOD NEXT TO WATER 49

CHAPTER 10: BUGGING IN AND HOME DEFENSE 58

CHAPTER 11: PREPARE FOR ANY DISASTER 64

CHAPTER 12: FUTURE-FOCUSED THINKING 87

CHAPTER 13: DISTILLING ALCOHOL FOR SURVIVAL 91

CHAPTER 14: SELF-DEFENSE AND WEAPONS 110

CHAPTER 15: TIPS, TRICKS AND HACKS 124

CHAPTER 16: A PREPPER'S SUPPLY CHECKLIST 128

CHAPTER 17: BARTERING ITEMS.................................... 161

CHAPTER 18: TIPS FOR STAYING ALIVE IN URBAN CHAOS
.... 165

CHAPTER 19: SURVIVAL KNIFE...................................... 168

CONCLUSION.. 195

Chapter 1: Definitions

This chapter is focused on defining the words that make up the prepping and survival field.

What is Prepping?

The Oxford dictionary defines prepping as the act of preparing for something; it further describes it as the practice of making active preparations for a possible catastrophic disaster or emergency, typically by stockpiling food, ammunition, and other supplies.

Simply put, prepping is the preparation you put in place for a wide range of emergencies.

Prepping has evolved to be more than a practice for some people; it has become a lifestyle; these folks are constantly living a life that can run successfully outside the make of our modern society.

This is evident by simple practices such as growing their personal food garden, buying safety gear for different emergencies, and more. Preparation for survival or extreme emergencies would require you to be ready for:

A deficit in the food supply

Lack of protective tools

Inaccessibility of transport & communication channels

Shutdown of electricity

Other forms of emergencies. In early 2020, the COVID-19 viral pandemic was a major scare to most people. Some claim that the prepping industry wasn't prepared for this Novel Coronavirus outbreak.

I am of the opinion that the skill set and training the prepping industry have equipped preppers with is highly relevant to tackling such pandemics. Since emergencies share some common attributes, there is nothing to lose by being prepared for a disaster.

Given that emergencies vary in the degree of severity and what effect they pose to humanity, there has to be levels of preparation. Levels of prepping (preparedness) are sometimes gauged by the period of distress and the intensity or effect on society. Based on these factors, prepping levels range from basic preparedness for short periods to preparing for emergencies that extend up to a year.

Levels of Prepping

Basic preparedness is the first of four levels of prepping. It refers to a simple preparation for mild and short emergencies.

For example, most organizations would have a first aid kit in case of small cuts and injuries during work; other individuals have alternate plans in case of a blackout in their area. These preparations are made in case of mild emergencies, which are usually short-lived; there is nothing special about them, although the threat they pose would depend on the current situation.

The other three levels of prepping are not specifically named but are identified by the period of emergency.

The second level of prepping covers emergencies/ disasters that would have an effect for up to 30 days

The third level covers a period of three months or more

The fourth level covers catastrophic events that would affect you for almost a year

With each level comes some necessities and intense preparation. A disaster that affects communication networks would require you to find some other means of communication; you would also require defensive equipment against hostile neighbors looking for supplies.

Irrespective of the nature and period of the disaster, prepping must be centered on some necessities. I would like to call them the pillars of prepping; they are the essential things prepping must cover.

Pillars of Prepping

If these pillars are absent in any preparation for emergencies, they do not meet the basic goals of prepping.

The art of accessing supplies

One of the fundamentals of prepping is teaching you how to access or acquire necessary supplies. Supplies range from food items to shelter, and every other item required for sustenance during the period of emergency. Preppers usually live their life prepared for these occurrences; some of them grow their own food, or always buy in bulk for reserve.

Aside from having supplies in reserve for food and cash, a prepper usually has the equipment for various kinds of emergencies. These supplies could range for communication channels, to alternate methods of sustaining and protecting themselves. In a later section, I will dive into the subject of necessary supplies, and include a checklist of items preppers must have.

The art of skills acquisition

Preppers do not just have supplies to suffice them through and during disasters. Preppers have fine skillsets for survival. For example, a first aid kit is not of much use if you do not acquire the skills and knowledge to administer first aid correctly. Preppers learn a lot of skills for survival, ranging from self-defense, communication, and any skill specific to the disaster.

Supplies would sustain life and provide you with the necessary tools, but skills are the next determinant of your survival. For instance, in the event of a flood, being able to swim and hold your breath under water may give you a good chance of survival.

The Art of Building a Community

Building a community is indispensable in prepping. Clearly, we humans are not know-it-alls. There is surely a need to connect with like-minded folks. In the occurrence of a disaster, we would have aid and assistance from these people. By complementing one another, it would be easier to survive and prepare for crises.

In addition, people would feel more secure and optimistic about survival when they are in groups rather than on their own. Having a community of preppers also allows you to pool together your resources.

Why Prepping

Why prepping? When emergencies occur, it becomes a test of who is most prepared and able to overcome the challenges. One thing is certain, the fact that emergencies happen.

In the occurrence of Simple Disasters

Even in a simple disaster, many lives could be lost or exposed to danger due to a lack of preparation. Many people may not have the requisite information or skills to rescue themselves and others. You do not want to be amongst that group of people with zero ability to make a difference in a life or death scenario.

When you are left with no options

What do you do when you are left with no options in the event of an emergency? What happens when the structure of modern society collapses and makes help difficult to access? What happens when everyone, including the government, is too busy saving themselves to save you?

You may not have the luxury of time to wait for help and your country's support system. You may come to regret lacking simple survival skills, which could save your life in a crisis. It is better to be over-prepared than under-prepared!

Better Equipped!

In the occurrence of a disaster, you are better equipped to survive. When the anticipated disaster happens, you are confident of what to do. This would save you a lot of time and paranoia.

As much as people believe their instincts may come to their rescue during a disaster, they may turn out to be unreliable. Why depend on your instincts in trying times when you can arm yourself with knowledge and experience within a controlled environment?

Survival is a basic human Instinct

Survival is a basic human instinct; humans and animals constantly strive to survive and adapt to their environment.

Speedy Recovery

In the occurrence of a catastrophe, only people who have prior plans would be less affected. After the emergency has come and gone, they would still be able to continue life without experiencing too much of its negative impacts.

The signs are encouraging. A survey conducted in 2020 found that approximately 141 million Americans, or half the US population, are preparing for emergencies with a focus on doomsday[1].

Doomsday is the school of thought that believes that some sort of disaster could wipe out a country or a large chunk of the world. While that may be the worst-case scenario, the important question to ask is, how do you start prepping if you have totally no experience?

Chapter 2: The Purpose Of A Bugout Bag

One of the things that those new to prepping often confuse, is the purpose of a bugout bag. As a result, there's often a great deal of error that does into preparing a bugout bag. Rather than being the bag that contains all the resources you'll need for days on end, a bugout bag is intended to get you through the first 72 hours in a SHTF scenario. Your bugout bag will therefore serve as a temporary means of survival until you're able to get to your bugout location.

The majority of preppers will have their homes fully stocked for such an unfortunate event and thus, this will be the place that they're looking to head to. However, there may come a time where it is necessary to evacuate your home and thus, it's essential to have a backup plan in place- in the event that the safety and security of your home has been compromised. In such an instance, you'll once again, be in need of a bugout bag, that will serve the purpose of keeping you prepared with all the essentials you need to get from point A to point B.

Unless staying off the main roads is a necessity, it'll be easy for you to hop in your car and head to the next safe location. However, in the event that your car is one of the things that need to be abandoned and you've got no other option than to seek safety on foot, the supplies you have with you, will determine how easy or hard of a task you have ahead of you.

All in all, a bugout bag is not intended for long term survival and the reasons are obvious. Trudging around with a bag that contains half of your stockpile will be impossible and thus, the items that you pack need to be selected carefully. It is, therefore vital that you have a broad idea of what it is you're prepping for and plan accordingly. Frequently analyze the scenarios you may encounter as the more you do this, the more likely it will be for you to pick up on any essential items that you may have forgotten.

The weight of your bugout bag

Don't get lost in the masses of information

With so many lists on the internet, it's easy to get overwhelmed when trying to figure out what items you MUST include. However, once you've had a chance to take a step back and look at what's important for you, narrowing this list down will become significantly easier. Later on in this book, we'll go over 'must have items' as well as a few other items that may be necessary to one prepper or the other, based on the scenarios they're preparing for. A great deal of the gadgets that you'll come across are nice and flashy. However, it's very questionable how effective they'll be when you're trying to make a run for it. Be sure that no item in your bag, is there for the sole purpose of taking up space and being 'cool'.

Once you're able to come up with a list of items that are imperative to have, you'll find it significantly easier to ensure that your bugout bag isn't more of a trouble to carry than a potential lifesaver.

The 30% rule

As a rule of thumb, your bugout bag should not weigh in excess of 30% of your body weight. So, once you're done packing up all your supplies and filling your bag with all the things you think you'll want to do a quick check to see if your bugout bag falls into the right weight category.

Of course, there are numerous ways to cut down on the weight of your bugout bag and the following chapter will take a look at ways in which you can have a lighter bugout bag but not a less than sufficient one.

Remember, you'll want to get from point A to point B as quickly as possible and the heavier the load you have to carry, the harder this task becomes. Because sorting through your bugout bag in the face of a crisis will be counterproductive and trying to move quickly and hide with unnecessary bulk won't get you far, high importance needs to be placed on the weight of your bag.

Chapter 3: Sourcing Your Items Cheaply

You've set yourself a budget, but what do you buy? Don't panic, you've been grocery shopping before, probably in the last week. The easiest prepping is done without doing anything special. With the economic problems many families are facing sourcing things cheaply is a common pastime. The most obvious item you'll want a lot of is food, and food doesn't come cheap.

To find food cheaply you'll want stuff that has a long shelf life and a reasonable expectation that you'll actually eat it. 5Lb jars of pickles might be cheap but if you hate pickles why are you buying them? What you'll want to look at is foods that keep well, these include dried, pickled, or canned items. The cheapest of these is rice and beans which is why they are a staple for many preppers. When you're next in the grocery store you can find them for about $1 for a large bag, for $2 with some seasoning you've made a basic meal that can be stored uncooked for a while without having to worry that it will go bad. Pair this with a tin of chicken and you've got a decent dinner that can be heated without a lot of trouble for less than you probably spend on an instant meal. Any dried grains will work but white rice is a very calorie dense food which makes it good for survival purposes. Look at other dried foods available – lentils, peas, and even corn can be bought dry so that it can be cooked later. These take up much less weight and space than cans but still provide a good source of food.

Canned foods are another popular grocery store item; if you're budgeting already then you're probably familiar with the idea of store brands. Many stores offer their own version of brand name items at a significant discount. These discounts mean you may get 2 for 1 price on things you might already be buying. Consider doing just this, if you're going to pick up a can of corn, choose the cheaper store brand and get 2 instead and one can be saved for your stash. In addition to this many stores run specials such as getting 10/$10 or buy one get one free. Look out for these on your weekly shop to save money when adding to your food stash. Don't buy items simply because they are on sale, you'll waste your money; buy items that you will actually use on sale or they will simply sit on the shelf and go to waste if you don't need them.

The grocery store is an easy place to start when sourcing survival items, sales, coupons, and store brands are ideal ways to stretch your survival budget. If you've ever watched a show about couponing you know those people can save money and even make money just buying groceries. Start looking in your local paper and online for coupons you can use towards your weekly shop and survival needs. You can also consider getting membership to a wholesale club and buying in bulk for the same reason. Bulk items tend to be more expensive though so you'll probably be buying fewer items for the same price. If you're working slowly this isn't great if disaster strikes before you're ready but is ideal if you want to jump start with a bit more money and then build onto that. These clubs usually have specials and bonuses too. In addition some of the items end up being much cheaper than you will find in the grocery store. Salt for example comes in large boxes for less than $1 while in the grocery store half sized pots are three times that. This can save you money in your regular expenses that can then be put towards prepping.

Even if you're stretching your budget there might still be some things you need meanwhile, new clothes, running shoes etc. Rather than buying these new consider thriftless for them. Thrift stores are a marvelous resource for preppers as they can stretch your budget for everyday wants a little further and are often full of items that can be used for prepping. Many stores have boxes of pickling jars for pennies each that cost ten times that in the store new, old items like hand mixers that can be used with no power, and even brand new things that can be added to your stash like sleeping bags or blankets.

Similarly to thrifting Garage and estate sales are ideal for finding gently used or vintage items that can help you prep cheaper than buying new. Many people will start prepping and then find they don't want to devote time or they're looking to scale back a bit, or even those who have bought items and then upgraded. Often you can find the same old time stuff — manual hand mixers etc. at yard sales even cheaper than you would at a thrift store. Many of these older items were built to last and that's exactly what you want when finding tools and kitchen items.

There's often plenty of camping stuff at yard sales too. The only downside is that anything outdated might just be that – out of date. Be careful of anything that has an expiration date as you're risking your health and safety with items like this. Expired food and medicine isn't always dangerous but it's certainly not worth the risk just to save a bit of money.

Though you might not think that there would be anything at a dollar store that could help survival stockpiling you couldn't be more wrong. If you're looking to build up your stash cheap then dollar stores are ideal. You can often find brand name items cheap or items that can have multiple uses. For example a $1 shower curtain is just that, or it's a very cheap tarpaulin that could be ground cover in the case of bugging out. Some of the best things include antibiotic cream, bandages, and even some foods. Dollar stores are really a gold mine for getting small items that you may need to stock up on; their "serving" size of many items is also small enough that they are ideal to carry for bug out bags on the go.

Chapter 4: Water Storage

Survivalists practice something that is known as the Law of 3s. In a nutshell, it goes something like this.

3 hours to find shelter to maintain core body temperature

3 days to find water

3 weeks to find food

Water is going to be one of your top priorities when you are thrust into a survival situation. While you can live 3 days without water, it isn't something you will want to attempt. You will be uncomfortable, weak and dehydrated within the first day of not having water.

Because water is so important, you must do what you can to have a supply of water on hand. It would be great if the water was already clean and ready for you to drink, but that is not always feasible. You can clean water, but you cannot always find it. Do what you can to store water using one of the following methods.

Rain Barrels

You can use new, clean plastic garbage cans from Home Depot to make rain barrels. Check with local restaurants and bars and ask if you can buy their food-grade barrels. Food grade barrels tend to be blue or orange. NEVER use barrels that held chemicals. Catching water from the roof of your house is free and is a quick way to build up a healthy water storage.

Commercially Bottled Water

Buying cases of bottled water from your local grocery store is another option. Keep in mind this could get very expensive. Stacking cases of water is tricky as well. You risk the flimsy bottles smashing and your water leaking everywhere.

Large Cisterns

This is something you will see on farms and ranches. These cisterns can be small and hold 250 gallons of water or quite large and store 1000 gallons of water. These are excellent investments if you have the space to store the cistern.

Home-Bottled Water

You can certainly reuse containers to bottle your own water. Only use thick plastic bottles, like those that hold juice or soda. DO NOT use milk jugs. The plastic is thin and it will break down within a matter of months.

Swimming Pools/Hot Tubs

These are certainly options and they can hold thousands of gallons of water, but it should never be your first choice. The water in pools and hot tubs is treated with chemicals that can make a person very ill should they ingest them. If you will be using your pool as a backup water source, wait at least 3 days before you attempt to use it. This will give the chemicals time to evaporate.

When you are thinking about water storage, it is important to calculate how much water you need. The rule of thumb is every person in your household will need one gallon of water each day. This factors in the water needed for cooking and moderate bathing. It is not enough water for a bath or shower so make sure you add lots of deodorant to your emergency supply.

Chapter 5: How Important Is It To Be Physically Prepared For A Disaster?

Technology has taken over our lives to the point that living without our appliances, gadgets and knickknacks can seem not only hard but entirely impossible. When we are hit with a natural disaster or even a manmade one, the first thing that is usually is affected is power which makes all our electronic devices pretty much useless. We have become so dependent on power that when such a situation strikes us, we are lost not able to understand how to go on. During some disasters entire countries have to survive without power for up to a week.

During this time if you have physical skills and you have prepared yourself for such situations, you would have higher chances of survival. This is why only mental preparation will not help you get very far but physical skills will allow you to make the best use of resources at hand.

One of the biggest physical requirements that people lack these days is stamina. People tend to take transport for even the smallest distances which is why they no longer have the stamina to walk even a mile without feeling tired out. When it comes to survival you may have to walk for days to reach a safe house. The physical strains of this journey can make most people give up pretty soon. Taxis, buses or even trains will no longer be functional in times of survival which is why you should get into the habit of walking.

Start with the smallest distances such as walking to work or at least taking the stairs and building your stamina from there till you can walk for a good duration. Also get into the habit of carrying baggage while walking because you will need to carry supplies while you walk for miles in times of a disaster. Keep on increasing the weight you are carrying till you feel you are prepared for disaster survival.

Chapter 6: Preserving Fresh Foods

While most people resort to buying preserved food items in the grocery to prep their survival pantries, preserving fresh foods in own home is also a great way to increase your supplies. Home-preserved foods are generally more nutritious than commercially preserved foods, many of which contain substances that can be harmful to one's health if consumed in large amounts. Preserving your own foods may also cost you less, especially if you also grow produce from your own garden.

Self-preserving, however, may take you time and may require some special equipment. Listed here are the most basic and common ways to preserve your fresh foods.

Pickling

Pickling is a very old method of food preservation which uses vinegar and brine to facilitate anaerobic fermentation in food, thus preventing bacterial growth. Pickling requires food to be submerged in salt and vinegar solutions for long periods of time (usually for several days). It is important to follow pickling recipes properly in order to ensure the efficiency of preservation. Do not use table salt for brining; instead, use canning or pickling salt. Most recipes will also require you to use other spices like pepper to help fight bacterial growth. Pickled foods usually give off a strong, sweet and sour taste with deep flavour.

After pickling a food, proper canning and storage is necessary in order to ensure longevity of the product. Properly pickled and canned food can last anywhere between three to twelve months.

Canning

Many fresh foods require pressure canning or a special pressure canner equipment to keep them from spoilage. Foods with low acid content (pH greater than 4.6) like red meat, seafood, milk, poultry and most vegetables are canned using this method. Pressure canning requires high level of heat (up to 240 degrees Fahrenheit) to kill all forms of bacteria and properly sterilizing your product.

Hot water bath canning, however, can be used to can foods with high acidity (pH below 4.6). This includes jam, jellies, many fruit juices and pickled recipes.

The best cans to use for canning are reusable glass jars that seal tightly like Mason jars. Remember to sterilize the jars, lids and rings before canning.

To perform hot water bath canning, prepare your food as you regularly would with your chosen recipe. Place them into your jars and seal tightly.

Next, fill a large pot halfway with water and heat it to 140-180 degrees Fahrenheit. Using appropriate tongs, place your canned goods into the pot. Add more boiling water up to one inch above the now submerged jars, then bring the whole pot to a strong boil. As soon as it starts boiling, set the timer, cover the pot and reduce to a low boil for the time period as indicated by the recipe. When finished, carefully use tongs to remove the jars from the pot and let cool on a towel or cooling rack. Hot water bath canning is successful if sealed lids are concave after around 12-24 hours. These properly canned goods can last for a year.

Freezing

Frozen fruits and vegetables make good ingredients for baked goods and smoothies. They also make for a healthy snack especially since you don't have to add salt or artificial preservatives for this method. Freezing is by far the easiest method of preserving that you can do at home. Take note, however, that frozen foods won't last as long as other foods preserved through other methods, especially during a power outage. Nevertheless, it's a good way of making sure that you keep spare food available in your freezer.

Commonly frozen fruits and vegetables include bananas, cherries, berries, beans, broccoli, corn, carrots and peas.

To start, wash, core and skin your fruit as needed. Cut large fruits into slices or chunks for faster freezing. Soak them into lemon juice to keep them from browning when they freeze. Lay your dry fruit slices or chunks onto baking sheets, in such a way that they form a single layer and slices do not touch. Store them in the freezer for several hours. When fruits are completely frozen, store them in storage bags or containers, label and indicate storage date for reference.

Vegetables can be frozen the same way as fruits, but they also require a short boil.

Dehydrating

Moisture is one of the culprits of fast food spoilage. As such, dehydrating is another popular way of food preservation. It takes out all the moisture content from food, leaving no room for bacteria and mold to replicate. Meat, herbs, fruits and seeds are foods that are commonly dehydrated. Properly dehydrated foods can last around four months to a year. The big setback in dehydrating, however, is that getting rid of its moisture means getting rid of a large part of its nutritional content, as well.

Like pressure canning, dehydrating also requires a special equipment, the dehydrator. In essence, a dehydrator contains levels of stacking trays where you put your food in, and they are circulated by air that is moderated at just the right temperature – enough to pull the moisture out from the foods, but not enough to cook them.

Chapter 7: Food

Food is usually the first thing many beginning preppers think about. While it is certainly important, it isn't truly your main priority in a true survival situation. To help you understand your priorities in survival, check out the Law of 3s.

3 Hours to find sheltering

3 Days to find water

3 Weeks to find food

We already discussed shelter and we will discuss water next, but let's talk about food. Quite frankly, while these laws are technically true, nobody wants to go 3 weeks without eating! Think of how you feel after not eating breakfast or lunch. By the time dinner rolls around, you are starving, grumpy and maybe a little tired and shaky. Imagine not eating for days on end. What's worse is that in a survival situation you are going to be doing a lot more physical activity to survive. You may have to go out and gather water, hunt, chop wood or look for supplies. You need sustenance.

When you plan on storing food for an emergency, calories count. You want the most calories possible in a single serving of food. You are not worried so much about quantity, but quality.

Let's explain it like this; assume each person in your family needs 2,000 calories per day to survive. Honestly, that is a low number. Men would need a bit more to maintain their weight if they are doing a lot of physical activity, but 2,000 calories would sustain a person.

So, we will say 2,000 calories per person per day. Assume you have a family of 4. Now, you need 8,000 calories per day.

A standard #10 can of freeze dried food contains approximately 16 servings. Let's assume we are serving the family Creamy

Beef Stroganoff. Each serving contains 250 calories.

2000 (total calories needed)/250 (calories per serving) =8

Each family member would need 8 servings or half a #10 can of freeze-dried food.

With a family of 4, that means you would need 2 cans of food per day.

Assume you are building up a 30-day supply, 30 x 2=60.

You would need 60 #10 cans of stroganoff to keep the family fed for a month.

Now, that is just an example and you certainly wouldn't want to feed your family stroganoff for a month straight, but it can help you calculate the amount of food you need.

Freeze-dried food does tend to be more expensive. However, it can last up to 25 years. When stored in ideal conditions. You don't have to only store freeze-dried food. In fact, you wouldn't want to. It is far too costly to solely depend on freeze-dried food for your emergency supply.

You need to diversify your food storage. This will give you more options, which will make the family happier, as well as be easier on the budget. If you have a garden or can get to a farmer's market, buy produce in bulk and learn to can. Home-canning can save you a great deal of money.

The following is a basic list of food items you will want to include in your food storage.

Dried beans

Grains; whole wheat

Flour

Canned meats; salmon, chicken, tuna, Spam

Canned fruits

Canned vegetables

Freeze-dried dairy products

Pasta

Canned tomato sauce

Peanut butter

Crackers

Dehydrated fruits

Snacks

Freeze-dried meals

Canned chili, beans, etc...

This list is not conclusive, but it does give you a pretty basic idea of what to start storing. Dehydrated foods do take more water to reconstitute than freeze-dried. Keep the dehydrated foods to a minimum, except fruit, which you can eat without reconstituting.

The way you store your food will make a huge difference in the expected shelf life. Choose a place that meets all or at least most of the following criteria.

Not exposed to extreme heat or cold

Out of direct sunlight

Dry

Good ventilation

One of the challenges of an urban prepper is finding room to store your goods. You are going to have to get creative, but it can be done. Maximize every bit of space under the beds, under furniture and in closets. Consider building shelves around your upper wall area. This will give you a great deal of space for your food storage without using up any of your daily space.

Chapter 8: Essential Prepper's Medical/Sanitation Supplies

Living in a world that is without hospitals and doctors seems terrifying, but with the proper supplies and a little knowledge, you can take your health into your own hands.

Toilet paper

Sanitary products

Colloidal silver (natural antibiotic)

Thieves oil

Tea tree oil

Aspirin

Vodka

Baking soda

Bleach

First aid kit (with gauze, bandages, tweezers, thermometer)

Vitamins

Soap

Sunscreen

Dental care (mouthwash, floss, toothbrushes)

Mosquito netting

Insect repellant

The first item that always runs out during a crisis is toilet paper. Another essential sanitary item is feminine products. Stock up now while you still can and be prepared to barter.

When selecting medicinal items for your storeroom, think about worst-case scenarios. There won't be an emergency room or the antibiotics our bodies have become so used to getting. In fact, there be antibiotic-resistant diseases sweeping the globe, but let's assume that having some kind of treatment for bacterial infections is better than none.

Colloidal silver is a natural antibiotic and the only one you can get without a prescription. Doctors will likely not recommend it, but that's mostly because they can't prove the effectiveness of colloidal silver 100%, and they want you to get your medicines straight from them.

Another natural medicine is Thieves oil, which prevents and treats respiratory diseases. It is named after its original use during the Black Plague in Europe, when looters carried cloves and spices in their pockets while they robbed the dead. Their survival rate baffled the doctors at the time, but science now knows the ingredients in their pockets are what saved them.

Tea tree oil is another essential oil that when rubbed on the skin, can combat bacterial, fungal, and viral infections. It can be difficult to stock up on these two oils because they are expensive, but if you have the means, looking into buying essential oils instead of your run-of-the-mill cough syrups and pills is definitely worth your while.

This is not to say that you should neglect having a traditional first aid kit on hand. Your kit should include a painkiller like Aspirin, plenty of gauze and bandages, tweezers, and a non-mercury thermometer.

Vodka has several medical uses, like soothing a headache and treating blisters. It is also one of a few perfect bartering items since people will always want alcohol even (or especially) during an emergency.

In addition to being a useful deodorizing material, baking soda is a cheap and effective tooth cleaner, which will be necessary after tubes of toothpastes inevitably run out. Baking soda is also great as a nontoxic face cleanser when used in moderation. Bleach has a similar dual purpose, as it is a powerful surface cleaner and can be filtered into water to purify it.

The effectiveness of vitamins is constantly being debated, but some vitamins are certainly better than none, especially when nutrient-rich food is scarce. Vitamin D3 and E are especially useful as energy-boosters, and calcium will become important when there isn't milk readily available.

Keeping clean is the easiest way to fight bacteria and disease, so be sure to stock up on soaps for skin and clothes. Soap is easy to store and is a popular bartering item.

Sunscreen is going to become a crucial health item as modern society's cubicle lifestyle will be traded for one dominated by working outdoors in the sun. Long-term exposure to sun can cause skin cancer, so store sunscreen now while you can and learn some natural methods for protecting your skin.

Besides baking soda, gather toothpaste, toothbrushes, floss, and mouthwash. Dental kits will become important bartering items, and the longer you can brush your teeth with regular toothpaste, the more normal your routines will be.

With unknown and dangerous diseases on the rise, you will need to have some supplies to protect yourself from insects that carry these diseases (West Nile, malaria, etc). Having good mosquito netting is especially important if you plan on living outdoors. The same goes for insect spray, which can repel ticks as well as mosquitoes.

Chapter 9: Food Next to water

Next to water, the most important item to stock up on is food. Food sources are divided into what you store for the long term, fruits and vegetables you grow on your own from gardening, meat from livestock, and natural sources from what the wilderness provides.

Long Term Storage Food

This is food that you can store in the pantry for up to a year and it will still be perfectly fresh. At that point, you may want to consider rotating it out.

Canned Meat. It's certainly not as good tasting as a roast turkey or freshly caught fish, but canned meats like salmon, chicken or turkey will be some of the best sources of protein you can store for the long term. What's more is that you can store canned meat for up to two years and it won't go bad.

Canned Vegetables. We've all heard the phrase to "eat your green vegetables." It holds just as much, if not more, relevance in a survival situation. Canned vegetables like green beans and carrots will last long and provide your body with the nutrients it needs.

Cereal. As long as the box remains sealed, cereal is good for months if not years. Look for specific cereals that come packed with a variety of different grains.

Crackers (Whole Wheat). Whole wheat crackers can be improvised to make miniature sandwiches, but more importantly, they come packed with fiber and fat content. As long as the packaging remains unsealed, the crackers should be good for up to six months.

Dried Fruit. Think raisins, apricots and peaches. Dried fruits are full of fiber and potassium, and will last in storage for many months.

Granola Bars. We've all packed a granola bar in our pocket for a mountain hike or a bike ride one time or another. Granola bars are incredibly healthy, easy transportable, and filled with carbs. They won't go bad for over six months.

Nuts and Peanut Butter. If you have an allergy, you'll obviously want to avoid this one. However, peanut butter is one of the best sources there is for protein and fats, and both nuts and peanut butter provide much energy to the human body. They can be stored in the pantry for over a year and not lose any of their freshness.

Spices. Who says you can't add some flavor to the food you eat in a survival/prepping situation? Store essential spices like salt and pepper, sugar, or even Cayenne pepper. Spices are will also become very valuable items when it comes to bartering.

Fishing and Hunting

You'll have to learn to go traditional and live off the land if you run out of food at home. Unfortunately, deer hunting and fishing are actually harder than they sound, and require the utmost patience. Fortunately, the rewards for a successful hunting or fishing trip will be immensely gratifying.

The best advice that can be given about deer hunting is to find a spot rich in deer sign, such as tracks and feces, and lay hidden in wait at that location in the early morning hours and in the time before dusk when the deer are more active. When hunting smaller game, such as grouse and turkey, hunt in warmer weather in open country, and also in early morning or late afternoon hours. You can lure large and small game alike with calls.

You'll likely find more lucrative prospects for food by fishing in a river or a stream than you would hunting game cross country. Besides, fish are the best protein source available to you in the wilderness.

If you lack traditional fishing equipment, there are three alternative techniques you can try:

1. For the first technique, you can improvise to make fishing hooks and lures on your own. Clothing strands, wire, and vines make excellent fishing lines, while paper clips, soda can tabs, and needles will make for a fine hook. As a lure, use jewelry, colored cloth, or small bugs, worms or frogs that you catch on your own.

2. The second technique you can try is fishing with a net, which is more effective for catching schools of smaller or younger fish than it is for solitary big keepers. Anything such as a jacket, a towel or a blanket can be used as a net for fishing improvisation. Tie the two ends of your improvised net to two sticks, and then run the net through shallow areas where schools of fish are plentiful. Push the fish towards a dam or the embankment and

lift the net as soon as you think you have caught something.

3. Finally, the third improvised fishing technique is known as Weir fishing. In a stream or river, place three or more stakes in a large teepee shape and then close off two of the sides with whatever materials you have (rocks, cloth, more stakes, etc), with the open end facing upstream. Sit and wait for a fish to swim itself into the V, and then close off the open end of the V to trap your prey.

Livestock

Don't discount raising livestock for food. Small livestock, like chickens and rabbits, are very simple to take care of and give you great benefits in the way of food.

Chickens have been raised by humans across the world for thousands of years. Chicken hens yield a number of eggs every day, and you can always kill a chicken for its meat if times are desperate. To care for chickens, all you need is a well-constructed coop, some shelter for them to lay eggs, chicken feed, and water.

Chickens should be your first choice when it comes to livestock, and rabbits your second. Like chickens, all they need are a coop, some shelter, feed, and water. Female rabbits will produce multiple liters every year, with an average of eight kits per liter. With just a few mating pairs of rabbits in the coop, your family can have meat on the plate every other week.

Gardening

Invest as much of your time as possible into growing and maintaining your garden before disaster strikes, because when it does hit, you'll have less time to learn how to care for your garden.

You won't need a whole lot of space to plant crops in your garden. Even people who live in the cities can become self-sustainable by planting a garden on their front deck or even inside their home. But whether you plan on dedicating a portion of your backyard to gardening or just a space by the windowsill, the fundamentals of gardening remain the same.

Begin by constructing raised beds and position these beds so that your available space is used effectively. Next, select the plants that you'll want to use. Since the seasons change, different plants will grow in different seasons. However, all plants are divided into two basic kinds: hardy and non-hardy.

Hardy plants are made to grow in the fall and winter months as they can withstand cooler temperatures, but if grown outside, still require a greenhouse to protect them from the outside elements. Non-hardly plants can be grown in the spring and summer. When you purchase plants, they will almost always be labeled as either hardy or non-hardy.

As for what specific types of plants you should grow, beans, cabbage, corn, potatoes and squash will be the best choices. To get the most food out of your garden, your plants must receive the right amount of required water, sunlight, and fertilizer. You should thoroughly research each type of crop you plan to plant to ensure they are cared for properly.

Chapter 10: Bugging In And Home Defense

Now obviously for bugging in you will need provisions, but we have already covered that. In this chapter I will go over everything else you should consider when getting ready to bug in for the long haul.

Neighbors and Community

A big consideration when considering your bugging in plans are your neighbors. In a WROL situation, you can form a neighborhood support group with the people around you. This is much harder to do on the road as you won't know the people you are bumping into and many of them will most likely treat you as being hostile right away. You neighbors are far less likely to do this.

Some people may not get on with their neighbors but there is safety in numbers and it's much better than trying to go it alone seeing as you may need to defend yourself at some point. If you have group of people who are all willing to work as a group to defend your area from potential attackers you will be in a much better position.

Working with your neighbors has more than just defensive benefits. You can also share knowledge. Maybe one of your neighbors is a shortwave radio hobbyist and he can provide you with communications with other countries. Another neighbor may have a solar panel that you can use to power that radio when the grid goes down. So by coming together you can form a much more functional group with shared expertise in different areas.

You can also barter with them for supplies that you need. Or set up trade with other communities around you. If you do decide to bug out then you will lose this local support system.

Sanitation

Sanitation is another concern for those of us who are intending to bug in. In a situation of a magnitude we are discussing, all of the utilities we take for granted would stop working. People commonly think of electricity and gas but many people fail to consider sewage.

The amount of humans living in cities and towns with no sewage would cause major sanitation issues and health risks. Your toilet will still flush if you pour a bucket of water down the bowl but who has all of that water to waste in a disaster situation?

Latrines are the most likely solution to this problem but I expect some people will still just throw their waste out onto the street or down the drains that will quickly become blocked with no maintenance. So use the toilet if you have the water to spare, if not then you're going to have to dig a latrine.

You can wash with very small amounts of water and you should keep spare soap, shampoo and tooth paste. This is something a lot of people forget when getting their survival supplies together. If you keep enough of these items you will most likely be able to trade them as they will be considered a real luxury before long.

Home Defense

You should also think about how you would defend your home in a bug in situation. This depends on the type of properly you live in along with the layout and the surrounding area. So you will have to consider the implications of these things carefully.

The most obvious thing to consider is securing your home against intruders. In my previous book about home defense I recommended two great products to look at for securing your external doors called the OnGARD and the Nightlock (US link) door braces. Both are great for securing exterior doors such and preventing intruders from breaking in via your front and back door.

For interior doors, you're not going to be able to secure them quite as well as your external doors but the Buddybar Door Jammers (US link) are great for buying you some extra time by jamming a door shut if someone does get inside. There are cheaper versions of the product available but they aren't as strong and they are more liable to just slip out of the way.

The other obvious way of protecting your home is by using weaponry, which I will go into later on in the book. But one thing that will give you a huge advantage if it does come to combat is night vision googles. You have to remember that with the grid down in most scenarios, there will be very little light at night, even in towns and cities. If an intruder want's to loot your house under the cover of darkness, they will be doing so by moonlight alone unless they want to use a flashlight and stand out like a sore thumb. So the night vision will give you a distinct advantage.

The only problem is they are fairly pricey. Something like Yukon NV Goggles (US link – UK link) are a really pro bit of kit, but they are pretty expensive. Although these will allow you to see with fairly normal depth perception even at close quarters. Or you could go for something a lot more affordable like the Polaris Explorer Monocular (US link). This will basically allow you to use it like night vision binoculars and see what's going on around your home at night but it can't be used in close quarters due to the magnification.

Chapter 11: Prepare For Any Disaster

100 Tips and Tricks on How to Prepare Your Family for Disaster

At this point you've made you survival arrangement and made your stockpile list. Here are 100 tips and traps on the most proficient method to get arranged if there should be an occurrence of a SHTF circumstance.

1. Introduce security around your property. Secure your entryways and windows. Add strike plates to your outside entryways and include some spiked metal around your border.

2. Have vehicles put away securely where you can get to them rapidly.

3. Have a bug out arrangement set up with different leave courses arranged. Have a simple approach to get to your bug out

sacks on the off chance that you have to leave rapidly.

4. Have more than one area you can go to in the event that a specific range gets traded off, and you can no longer achieve it. I recommend having stockpiles begun in each of those areas.

5. Take in all the basic instincts I examined in the last part. Learning is power when you just have yourself to depend on.

6. Practice your medical aid aptitudes. The more you utilize them the more they'll get to be distinctly similar to second nature.

7. Work on utilizing your weapons. Run wellbeing drills, and go the terminating reach to always sharpen your abilities.

8. Hold crisis drills. Being quiet in a crisis can mean the contrast amongst surviving and not surviving. The most ideal approach to remain quiet is to know your leave procedures down frosty. Boring month to month will permit you to realize

what works, what doesn't, and will likewise get you used to irritating out in a rush. I hold drills at various circumstances of the day and night to keep my family reeling. You need your drills to feel reasonable.

9. Keep your arrangements private. Try not to circle in many people about your preparing plans. Those same individuals may come and attempt and take your prepares in a crisis circumstance. Try not to give anybody yet your gathering your SHTF stockpile area or your last bug-out areas.

10. Continuously continue preparing. Your work is never done. There is dependably a superior, more productive approach to get things done. That, as well as you'll have to turn in new prepares incidentally before old prepares lapse.

11. Utilize pastels as a crisis flame.

12. You can utilize bathroom tissue and channel tape to make a support that will set broken bones.

13. You can battle off frostbite by applying child oil to your skin.

14. Spare all your vacant water bottles for additional water stockpiling. Particularly great on the off chance that you have to travel, and need littler compartments to hold water in.

15. Begin fabricating your prepper library now. It's a smart thought to attempt and stock up on DIY books and how to guides. On the off chance that you don't know how to accomplish something these books can walk you through the issue and give you some required answers.

16. Begin interfacing with different preppers in your general vicinity and manufacture a group. It's less demanding to do things when you have similarly invested individuals who can offer assistance.

17. Begin trading some of your cash every month for valuable metals. In the event that society breakdown paper cash will have no esteem yet individuals will at present trade with silver, gold, precious stones, nourishment and supplies.

18. Make a protected place to store ice. This will permit you to store meat and different perishables for a more drawn out period amid the winter months without agonizing over creatures getting into it.

19. Keep your generator in a protected and very much monitored territory. These are difficult to disguise when running, and will be the objective of hoodlums in your area. Just run the generator when fundamental so as not to draw excessively undesirable consideration.

20. Putting away seeds are incredible, however products can bomb so don't just store seeds. Ensure you have a full preppers wash room just on the off chance

that you're garden sets aside some additional opportunity to go ahead.

21. In case you're bug out arrangement includes a great deal of strolling. You have to begin getting into shape now. Strolling for long separations with a 30lb + bug out sack on your back is a formula for over effort and potentially more terrible. To live off the network you should be in great physical condition. It's diligent work doing everything yourself!

22. Begin putting away kindling now! You require a huge wellspring of dry kindling to keep your home warmed and fire going long haul. Having an extensive supply of kindling close by will make life somewhat less upsetting. You additionally need to have a dry range to store your wood.

23. Perform consistent upkeep on your home, vehicles and weapons. Nobody knows when a fiasco will strike, so make a point to remain on top of any issues with your most vital resources. The exact

opposite thing you need is to give things a chance to fall into dilapidation just before SHTF.

24. Heating pop and preparing powder work for a huge amount of things. Utilize them to wipe out smells, evacuate recolors and to scour your ledges and sinks with.

25. You can utilize 5-gallon pails to effortlessly make a chicken water and feeder.

26. You can blend apple juice with your creature's nourishment or water to help their resistance.

27. Utilize some dark plastic sheeting so as to warm up a region of soil for some planting.

28. You can jab gaps in the covers of gallon containers and utilize them as watering jars.

29. Figure out how to introduce your fence without digging into the ground. Which is

extremely helpful in rough zones or in regions with extensive root frameworks.

30. Solidify your eggs to keep them from going spoiled.

31. You can utilize channel tape to help you open containers effectively.

32. You can utilize parts from an old bicycle to make a crossbow.

33. Spare your espresso beans. They can be utilized as a part of your fertilizer, they can be utilized as plant sustenance, they can be utilized as a part of cooking, and they can be utilized to freshen up your hands or refrigerator in the wake of managing smellier things like onions or fish.

34. 2 Liter pop containers are extraordinary for putting away rice and beans in.

35. You can utilize lightweight branches and a covering to make a flatboat.

36. You can make an alternative light out of a container of Crisco.

37. Chips like Doritos can make extraordinary tinder in the event that you have to begin a fire when absolutely necessary.

38. You can slice gaps in rubbish packs to make a brisk rain coat.

39. You can utilize your eyeglasses to amplify the sun and begin a fire with your tinder.

40. Try not to store water in old drain containers. It's difficult to wipe out the whole drain deposit and that can prompt to risky microbes starting to frame in your water.

41. Have various reserves for your prepping. On the off chance that you store every one of your prepares in one place and it gets traded off you'll have nothing to fall back on.

42. Remember about preparing for your pets. Many individuals inadvertently disregard this one.

43. Continuously test everything yourself. That goes for your whole weapons stockpile, and in addition any apparatuses or different things you have put away. You would prefer not to keep running into a circumstance where something is broken at the time it's generally required.

44. Purchase a couple bikes and little trailers you can append to them. This will make it simple to get a few supplies moved around your property or forward and backward from neighbors.

45. Know your neighborhood and state laws. In my town, there's a mandate against putting away more than 2 ropes of kindling. While you need to get readied you would prefer not to get fined or stuck in an unfortunate situation with the law while doing it.

46. On the off chance that your Zippo lighter comes up short on fuel you can in any case make a fire utilizing it. Take the cotton inside the lighter, utilize its rock to make a start and touch off the cotton.

47. Continuously convey some aluminum thwart on you. It is incredible for lying on the wet ground so as to make a dry stage to manufacture a fire.

48. Put covering tape on your electric lamp focal point to decrease your profile to others yet at the same time have enough light to get your assignment finished.

49. Figure out how to explore around evening time by utilizing only the stars. Just by taking in a couple of star groupings you can without much of a stretch make sense of the bearing you're going in.

50. In case you're not ready to manage the cost of a cut safe vest you can utilize a natively constructed vest with carbon steel saws. Simply consolidate a cluster of saws utilizing pipe tape as a part of request to

make a wound verification plate you can put in a vest for included insurance.

51. Fade can cleanse your water. The required proportion is 2 drops of unscented blanch to decontaminate one liter of water.

52. You can utilize toothpaste with a specific end goal to treat bug stings and bug nibbles.

53. You can lay tent pegs crosswise over two logs and transform it into a stopgap flame broil.

54. You can utilize only a thistle, a can, and a tiny bit of string as an angling pack when you're stuck a spot.

55. In case you're in wet conditions you can without much of a stretch get tinder by shaving off a few strips from the bark of logs and twigs.

56. Put huge shakes around a fire to assimilate warm. Notwithstanding when your fire starts to fade away the stones

will even now transmit warmth to keep you warm. You can likewise put the stones in the water to bubble and decontaminate your water.

57. You can include the unpalatable odor from some water by adding charcoal to the water while it's being bubbled.

58. Conduit tape a thwart cover within your canvas shield when out in the forested areas to expand the warmth in your safe house.

59. At the point when far from your home convey shine sticks. They can be fixing to some paracord and swung around to make an expansive circle of light on the off chance that stranded and should be saved by your gathering.

60. Dispensable ponchos are incredible as rain coats as well as transitory safe houses, and can likewise be transformed into a sun based still to help you get together and cleanse water.

61. Continuously keep some water decontamination tablets on you in the event that you can't begin a fire to heat up some water.

62. Try not to utilize untreated water to clean your injuries. Likewise don't run your hands through untreated water on the off chance that you have brushes or cuts on them.

63. You can utilize creature insides as draw for your catches, traps, and angling trips.

64. Continuously prepare your amusement far from your home as not to pull in any undesirable predators to your doorstep.

65. If at any time stung however some stinging brambles battle the corrosive infused by their needles by spitting on region immediately and scouring it hard with your apparel to get the corrosive out and off you.

66. You don't have to squander your vitality and time hacking each log with a

cleaver or hatchet. Simply kick them, and snap them utilizing power. Unless it's for furniture they don't should be great.

67. Continuously convey some type of trade with you out your bug out pack. For no less than a brief span money will in any case be an acknowledged type of coin.

68. At the point when ensuring not to lay on the ground. It will drain the warmth out of your body. Rather make a little stage out of sticks or logs and place your resting pack on top of that. It will help you hold required body warm.

69. When you gather your pack dependably put your light hardware on the base and heavier stuff on the top with a specific end goal to keep up a decent focus of gravity.

70. In case will do a great deal of physical movement wear less apparel. For whatever length of time that you're in constant movement and dry, you can drop every one of your layers and still be

agreeable. You would prefer not to sweat in cool climate as this will make your garments wet, and can prompt to hypothermia.

71. Convey a few cigarettes regardless of the possibility that you're not a smoker. It can be useful when around other individuals to help you make another companion or quiet somebody down.

72. Smoke is additionally a characteristic anti-agents for creepy crawlies. You can wave around your coat and other apparatus in the smoke with a specific end goal to keep yourself from getting eaten alive by ants and mosquitoes.

73. Socks can make great channels for getting earth and other poo out of water.

74. When you get a rankle, utilize a needle, and string it through your rankle with a specific end goal to deplete it. The string will keep the openings you made open, and douse up some other dampness. At that point put channel tape

over your rankle to dispense with erosion and any new rankles from beginning to frame.

75. Try not to drink a considerable measure of water when on a void stomach. It will disturb your bodies electrolytes and can bring about stun in extraordinary cases.

76. Continuously set up camp on hoisted ground and far from water. Water draws more bugs, and can prompt to you getting eaten alive during the evening.

77. Stay away from tobacco! Tobacco will diminish your stamina. It restrains your blood and oxygen stream to the mind. It likewise backs off blood thickening and mending by wrecking a portion of the platelets that are in your blood.

78. Because you see a creature drinking from a wellspring of water does not make it safe. Numerous creatures can drink and eat things hazardous to people.

79. Just drink the drain out of green coconuts. The drain out of more seasoned or even ready coconuts contains more oil that can go about as diuretic. This can prompt to lack of hydration from an episode of looseness of the bowels.

80. In the event that you ever lose your cleaver or blade you can make yourself a sharp edge by basically crushing together 2 rocks.

81. Figure out how to waterproof all your apparatus.

82. Figure out how to speak with your family or gathering utilizing hand flags so you can convey peacefully if important.

83. Take washes utilizing water. Try not to squander your put away water on remaining clean.

84. Continuously rapidly discard your waste. In case you're not apprehensive of pulling in consideration you can blaze it. Else, you have to truck it to another area.

Giving your refuse a chance to heap up will pull in bugs and rodents.

85. Dunk cotton balls into petroleum jam and after that store in little baggies. They can make extraordinary fire starters when out in nature.

86. Begin a small lumberyard. Stocks up on timber now so not far off when SHTF you'll have a supply of good wood to use on any ventures you have to build yourself.

87. Before settling your bug out pack do a dry run bearing it your home. Time yourself to perceive to what extent you can before need to put it down. On the off chance that you can't go long then you have to ease the burden.

88. Keep a running number of your ammo. You would prefer not to begin running low before a SHTF circumstance.

89. Have some Walkie Talkies put away so you can convey over short separations

with your gathering. This will prove to be useful frequently.

90. On the off chance that you live in a city and SHTF circumstance happens you're best wagered is to get out as fast as could be expected under the circumstances. Surviving long haul in a city is a perilous recommendation. You're best wagered is to have your bug out area in a more country zone. You need to get out before every one of the ways out get stuck up or cut off.

91. Start to cleanse your superfluous assets. You require however much space as could be expected for prepares and supplies. Begin assessing and eliminating things that aren't vital or increase the value of your family.

92. Assign a typical contact. On the off chance that you get split up amid a crisis and can't locate each other at your rally calls attention to bug out area have a man you can leave word with on your area. This

won't work in all circumstances however in instances of storms or littler fiascos having a man out of the hazardous situation you can all contact will help you remain in contact with each other until request is reestablished.

93. In a crisis circumstance you can utilize superglue to seal up any injuries you have.

94. At the point when introducing a peephole in your entryway be keen about where you put it. I propose putting it by the side of the entryways close to the doorknob that way you can keep your body behind the entryway on the off chance that the individual outside has a firearm.

95. Have a consistently convey pack on you. This is a couple of things that can fit in your pockets like a folding knife, multi-device, money, and a lighter. On the off chance that you convey a sack you may need to likewise incorporate a spotlight and a little convenient radio.

96. At the point when bothering out don't dress like a prepper. Dress coolly so you don't draw in as much consideration. On the off chance that individuals believe you're a prepper it will make you an objective for cheats.

97. When you're pestering out and are in uncertainty, continue moving. Try not to stay some place in case you're not feeling safe. Heed your gut feelings.

98. Make arrangements for various sorts of crisis circumstances. Every kind of SHTF circumstance can require its own particular arrangement and escape course. Set aside the opportunity to make anticipates the greatest number of significant situations as you can consider. You would prefer not to do this work preparing and have it be to no end, because of absence of arranging.

99. Make sense of a decent framework for disposing of your lavatory squander. You

need to have an arrangement for this set up before you require it.

100. Discover time to make the most of your life and your time with family. Living off lattice is diligent work, you have to make the most of your life keeping in mind the end goal to make all that you're experiencing justified, despite all the trouble.

Chapter 12: Future-Focused Thinking

The defining psychological characteristic of preppers is that they are always thinking about the future. Stage five is when it is clear that society is not going back to the way it used to be - at least for a long time - and those who have been preparing all along are going to be the most comfortable with this. It should be noted that what is discussed in this chapter are things all good preppers have been thinking about since they started their prepping journey, but stage five is when these thoughts start turning into reality.

The first concern all preppers run into is how to replenish their stockpile. Eventually, your food and water will start to run short. Are you going to barter? Live off the land? Location to some extent will decide this for you. If you live in a rural area, you have access to streams, lakes, and rivers with water you can either safely drink or run through a water filter. In a city, that is not so much an option, so you either move or rely on bartering. Eventually, all cities will likely be abandoned in favor of the wilderness, where people will begin to hunt and farm for their food. A good prepper will know this and prepare accordingly by stocking up on seeds, hunting equipment, and knowledge. Knowledge is arguably the most important "item" that all preppers can acquire. Bartering your services for goods is an ideal scenario as it costs you nothing and you get something in return. Skills like carpentry and sewing are also essential in building and repairing shelters, and making clothes, as eventually all existing clothing will wear out. Good preppers will be acquiring and honing new skills right along with stockpiling physical goods even before a SHTF scenario.

Another thing preppers will be thinking about is what the establishment of order will come to look like. With the government and police gone, chaos is sure to follow. Natural leaders always emerge, but just because someone has leadership skills, does not mean they will make a good leader. Preppers will be anticipating their choices if their area/city/commune come under leadership they do not agree with. Will they form a group and work with the leadership to make changes? Or will they just pack up and leave? What if the situation becomes violent? As a rule of thumb, the larger the group is, the more likely it is to become violent. Crowd-mentality is a very dangerous thing and toss in some desperate times and desperate people, and you have the recipe for disaster. To stay safe and keep order, it is likely that most peace-looking people will go their own way and make small villages. Especially-prepared preppers probably already have people in mind whom they would like to live by. This way, they can build trusting relationships, organize markets for bartering, community farms, and strong defenses to protect their group from violent, chaos-driven crowds.

Chapter 13: Distilling Alcohol For Survival

The ability to distil liquids in general is a skill that every serious survivalist should learn, without exception. Distilling alcohol in particular is a critical skill to learn because of the wide variety of purposes alcohol serves in a survival situation. Not only can it be used as a drink to lift your morale, but it can also be used as a means to start a fire or as a medical disinfectant.

You should be warned up front, distilling alcohol is a longer process than distilling water. But the good news is that once you learn the process and practice it, you'll know how to do it for the rest of the life.

Currently in the United States, you are only allowed to distill a limited amount of alcohol each year (two hundred gallons to be exact). But of course, in a long term disaster or chaotic survival scenario, this rule is heavily unlikely to be enforced.

For these reasons, distilling alcohol is not only a valuable skill to learn for survival, but it's also a valuable life skill in general to learn as well. In this article, we will cover everything you need to know about the art of distilling as a survival skill:

HOW TO CONSTRUCT A STILL

To begin to distill alcohol, you will need to create a still. The materials you need for this include the following:

-Bucket

-Boiling Pot

-Condensing Coil (preferably copper)

-Fire

-Rubber O-Ring

Use your rubber O-ring to seal off the pot; this will then allow you to move around the still and even open it but without sacrificing its airtight quality. While the bottom part of the pot will be treated just like any ordinary pot, the top part will need to be completely sealed off, with the exception of a single point for the gas to escape.

This is where the condensing oil comes in. The condensing oil will need to wrap around the pot and then down into a separate condensing tank or bucket filled with cool water. This is what will cause the evaporated alcohol to revert to its liquid form. Install the spout after this and your still setup is ready to go.

Before we proceed, it's important to note that your still needs to be as clean as possible before beginning in the distillation process. This isn't just so that the alcohol will turn out better, it's also for safety reasons and to reduce the chance of contaminants getting into your distilled alcohol.

HOW TO DISTILL ALCOHOL

Now that your still has been constructed, the fun part of this project begins: distilling actual alcohol.

Being by taking corn and placing it into a pot filled with warm water. Give the corn three to four days, it should begin to sprout. Once the sprout has reached two inches, you will be ready to proceed with the rest of the project.

Once the corn has sprouted, allow it to dry. Once it has dried, you can then grind down the sprouted corn into a cornmeal.

Once you have created the cornmeal, the time has come to make it into a mash.

Take a pot of boiling water and pour the cornmeal into it; put in yeast as well for added effect (a general rule of thumb to follow is one ounce of yeast for every six pounds of mash).

Some survivalists also like to add sugar to sweeten the taste, though it is not necessary. Adding sugar will not inhibit the fermentation process in any way, so it's entire up to you.

Give the fermentation process at least three days before proceeding on with the rest of the project. At the end of the fermentation process, check to see if it is bubbling. If it isn't, this signals that it is time to officially begin distilling. If it is, this means that the fermentation process is not yet over.

Fill up the still you built previously and transfer your mash over to it. Seal off the pot and then run your condenser coil through the bucket. Connect your spout.

The alcohol will start to vaporize once it has reached a temperature of a hundred and seventy three degrees Fahrenheit. At this temperature, the alcohol will start to evaporate from your mash and enter the condensing coil.

It will then travel through your coil and exit through the spout and into the bucket.

A huge and potentially fatal rookie mistake at this point in the process is to immediately drink this first 'batch' of distilled alcohol. Whatever you do, DO NOT DRINK IT because it will KILL YOU. The reason for this is because this liquid is one hundred percent alcohol and is further full of harmful contaminants. Even if it doesn't kill you, it will make you incredibly sick for a long period of time.

Instead, remove all of the initial liquid that forms. Continue this process by following the same steps above again, and the next jars should be safe to drink. At that point, there's nothing to stop you from distilling all of the alcohol that you want.

It's still a good idea to have an alcohol proofing device on hand that will let you know the percentage of alcohol in the liquid. As we just mentioned, 100% alcohol or anything close to that is not safe to drink whatsoever.

As you can probably tell, distilling alcohol is a relatively simple process but also one with multiple steps. If you've never distilled alcohol before, it's a wise idea to first work with someone who is highly experienced at it purely for safety reasons. You'll learn a lot from them and you can also avoid many of the mistakes that rookies make.

Also remember that, legally wise, you cannot sell alcohol in the United States without a license and you are limited to distilling two hundred gallons a year for your personal use.

Make Your Own Soap

When you think of survival, what are the priorities that come to mind first? You probably think of the need to find water, build a fire, and construct a shelter, right? You may also think of the need to learn proper first aid techniques, wilderness navigation techniques, and self-defense.

All of these things are vitally important for survival, but there's one more priority that you need to make sure is high on your list: personal hygiene. Maintaining proper cleanliness in a survival situation is critical when it's you against the elements and when sanitation standards drop (and they will in a disaster situation). You have to keep yourself clean if you want to avoid or resist disease and infection.

Obviously this means that you should include proper hygiene items in your survival kit, but it also means you need to make sure you know how to make personal hygiene items in the event that you run out of or don't have any of those items with you.

Soap is easily one of the most important personal hygiene items to have and it's also one of the easiest to make. Soap, in some form or another, has been used by humans for thousands of years due to its incredibly cleaning abilities. All that soap does is take insoluble particles and make them become soluble, so that water can then rinse those particles away.

You can also make soap with little more than animal fat, water, and ash. This is because the fatty acids in the animal fat will mix with the alkali in the ash, and the alkali will force the fatty acids to split and merge with the potassium in the alkali. This creates potassium hydroxide that is the foundation for soap.

In this article, we will walk you through the ingredients you need to have and the steps you need to undertake in order to make your own DIY survival soap:

INGREDIENTS

- Clean Water
- Wood Ash
- Animal Fat
- Plant Oil

- Salt
- Gravel and Sand
- One Plastic Container
- One Metal Container
- Knife

DIRECTIONS

- Take the plastic container and use a knife to punch several small holes through the bottom

- Place a layer of gravel into the container roughly an inch deep

- Pour another inch layer of sand over the gravel

- Fill up the rest of the container with ashes from your campfire

- Take the metal container and place it underneath the plastic container

- Slowly but steadily our your clean water through the plastic bowl so that it exits through the holes and pours into the metal container; the water will appear to be a dark grey or brown color, but this is exactly what you want (if the water starts to become more clear, you need to add more ash)

- This action will result in lye in your metal container. Boil this lye water until just over half of the lye water has been evaporated.

- Now add a cup and a half of animal fat into the lye water mixture. Stir and cook for at least thirty minutes. NOTE: your animal fat must be pure and free of all meat and blood. If it isn't pure, your soap will not turn out the way it should.

- You can now begin to pour your mixture into molds. The shape and size of the mold is irrelevant and totally up to you. You can carve a mold in the wood of a tree

- Allow the mixture to sit and dry in the molds for at least two days. It should slip right out of the molds when finished. At this point, you can either leave the mold as it is or you can use a knife or metal wire to cut it up into smaller pieces.

That's it! Pretty simple, right? While this DIY survival soap may not look or smell as nice as the soap you have in your bathroom right now, it will work just as good. You can always enhance the quality of the smell by adding essential oils into the mixture if you have any; lavender, lemon juice, and wintergreen are examples of oils you can add to add rich smells to your soap.

Escaping from A City

When people think of natural disaster, economic collapses, or terrorist attacks, large cities and urban centers are usually what come to mind first. Why? Because any kind of a disaster will always be more devastating in a more densely populated area because it not only affects far more people than in rural regions, but it also creates absolute chaos as well.

Knowing this, you may believe that all is lost for you when disaster strikes if you live in a city. But here's the truth: you don't have to stay in the city. If the disaster is bad enough that you determine bugging out if safer than bugging in, you should always be prepared to evacuate.

Nonetheless, you still need to have a proper plan and supplies in place for evacuating or else bugging out could be equally as risky as bugging in.

Have a Strategy

If you wake up one morning to see that chaos has engulfed your city and you have no plan, and if you decide to bug out as a result, chances are good that you'll either be killed in the open city or otherwise be stuck there in traffic. This is why it's so important to have a series of plans already set in place so you know exactly where you need to go when you need to evacuate.

Here are two things you need to ask yourself when coming up with an evacuation plan:

·Where Will You Go?

-You need to have a bug out location or at least a rendezvous point outside of the city where you'll either go or meet up with other people. Many preppers have friends or family living outside of the city and request permission to use their home in the event of an emergency. What's important is that the bug out point is within driving distance of the city so that you can realistically make it on your current tank of gasoline.

·How Will You Exit the City?

-The answer to this question is even more crucial. Even if you have one route already mapped out, you need to be prepared for the fact that that route will become cut off either due to heavy traffic or law enforcement road blocks. Always have a backup route that you can turn to, and a backup route to the backup route, and so on. Knowing your city's roads inside and out will definitely come in handy here.

Get Prepared

Easily the most important piece of gear for bugging out of a city is going to be your bug out vehicle. Your bug out vehicle can either be the vehicle that you drive every day, or it can be a vehicle that you have set aside in your driveway that you use exclusively for emergencies.

Regardless, there are several qualities that you need to include in your bug out vehicle including:

-Be able to carry your entire family and all of your supplies

-Be AWD/4WD and be able to drive over rough terrain

-Be able to hold extra fuel

-Be well maintained and reliable

There are specific things that you will need to carry in your bug out vehicle as well, including:

-20-40 extra gallons of gasoline

-7 gallons of clean water

-1 bug out bag per family member (small children excluded)

In addition, it's also a smart idea to carry weapons in your vehicle as well. Even if you don't like the idea of carrying firearms with you if you have small children with you, just know that you may have to face raiders or burglars who want what's in your vehicle and will threaten your family for it. A city in chaos is going to be a very dangerous place, so bringing weapons with you is critical.

How to Pre-Select Escape Routes

Easily the best way to pre-select escape routes out of the city will be to use online mapping software that utilize satellite imagery to show you all of the roads leading out of the city in addition to the surrounding terrain and any important landmarks.

At the bare minimum, you need to have at least three escape routes leading out of the city, and each route needs to be accessible to the other so that you can fall back on one in the event that one becomes cut off.

Avoid tunnels, bridges, and elevated highways if possible in your escape route because they are the points that will become the most congested in a the midst of a mass city evacuation. Furthermore, these points will also be the easiest targets for looters and burglars, so avoid them at all costs.

How to Decide When You Leave?

Finally, you have to be prepared to make the decision to leave in the first place. If the authorities have declared that all residents in the city are required to evacuate, then obviously you will have to do so. However, evacuating while the rest of the city is also evacuating will be the most difficult time to leave because all of the roads are going to become clogged with traffic, which would make a timely escape impossible.

For this reason, you would be wiser to make the decision to bug out before a mass evacuation is called so you can avoid as much traffic as possible and get out of danger early on.

Let's say that you live on the coast and you receive word that a hurricane is headed your way and will impact the coastline in about two days. The authorities have issued warnings but they have not called an evacuation yet. Now would be the perfect time to leave because A. you know that your life is in danger if you decide to stay, and B. you know that the authorities may call for an evacuation anyway. This is an example of where you will want to observe the warning signs early on and make your escape before everyone else does.

Chapter 14: Self-Defense And Weapons

Hitting Where it Hurts

There are literally thousands of self-defense moves that you can learn depending on how you were attacked. However, there are only 9 points that you need to focus on hitting in order to disable an attacker. These will cause enough pain that it will give you plenty of time to get away.

For the points we are going to be looking at, it does not matter if you are skinny or even a body builder, all you need is the speed and momentum which you will get by moving forward as you strike and putting all of your weight in to each hit.

Eyes

They can not grab you if they can not see you. A good gouge to the eyes or even a poke are both extremely painful. When gouging at the eyes, use both thumbs and you will soon have the attacker tearing up in pain.

Ears

There are many nerve endings in the ear and it is incredibly painful when you yank down hard on the ears.

Nose

Again, this is another area with plenty of nerves. When striking the nose, use the heel of your hand to strike the nose. You could also use an elbow just as effectively.

Groin

A good kick here needs no explaining really but you could also use your knee, punch or even grab and yank down as hard as you can.

Knees

Knees are only meant to bend one way so you can take an attacker off his feet by kicking straight in to the knee or from the side.

Solar Plexus

The solar plexus is a big bundle of nerves located just behind the stomach. A punch or a kick here will knock the wind out of an attacker giving you time to escape. Remember to move forward and put all of your weight in to your strikes.

Ankles

The ankles are very fragile. Slam your foot down in to the ankle and you will knock your attacker off balance.

Throat

Any strike to the lower valley of the throat is going to be effective. This should only be used when you are in extreme danger as it is a very sensitive area.

The images below shows the vulnerable parts of the human body.

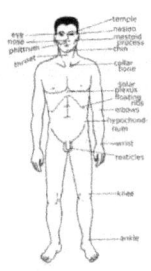

The Ankle Knockout

The world is full of weird things and when it comes to self-defense, nothing could be weirder than the ankle stop knockout. The good news about this move is that it does not matter how skinny or big you are, you can effectively use this move to crumple even the biggest of wannabe thugs.

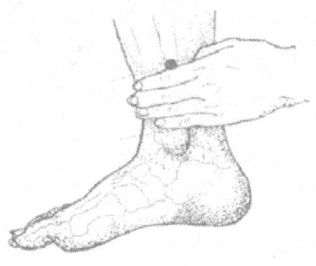

There is a hidden pressure point which is called the "Spleen 6" which is located about one hands width up from the ankle bone on the inside of the leg. You can see the placement in the image below.

You can see a quick video of the spleen 6 in the video at the following link:

https://www.youtube.com/watch?v=HPnbJy3tU8A

To knock the person out, you would need to stomp down in to the spleen 6 as hard as you possibly can. You need to try to hit it at a 45 degree angle and pretend that you are going right through the bone and in to the floor. By hitting the area hard, you will be making them feel so much pain that they should just pass out. If they don't pass out they wont be getting straight up which will give you enough time to make your escape.

It is important that you only use this when you truly feel like your life may be at risk.

It is extremely dangerous but can be used to end a fight very quickly.

Situational Awareness

To be more situationally aware, means to be more aware of your surroundings. Most people do not even realize just how vulnerable they actually are when they are doing their daily tasks such as grocery shopping or stopping off at the gas station. It can be learned by anybody who has the will and the discipline to do so.

Peripheral Vision

In most cases, people use their direct vision. They focus in front of them when out in public but it is our peripheral vision that needs to be used when out in public. We need to know what is happening around us at all times. You can practice this step by having a conversation with somebody at looking at their eyes but taking note of your peripheral vision.

The Automatic Scan

Everywhere we go, we naturally do what is called the automatic scan. We go somewhere and scan the area but are not really focused on the things that actually matter. Next time you go somewhere, pay attention to the following:

Where are the exits and how accessible are they.

Find barriers and see how you could avoid them to reach an exit point, or how you could use them to keep a potential threat on the other side.

If something does not look right such as an unattended bag, notify a worker of the space that you are in.

If somebody looks suspicious, take action to notify others and remove yourself from their direct path.

Watch your Back

Don't look over your shoulder. Instead, put your back against a wall to remove the possibility of somebody coming up behind you. This is good for crowded areas.

Using Reflective Surfaces to your Advantage

Reflective surfaces can be used to your advantage by showing you exactly what is going on behind you. If you are walking down the street you can use the display windows to see what is going on around you.

Stop and Pretend

If you feel like somebody is following you. Stop, turn around, and pretend that you went the wrong way. Let the person pass you. You can soon confirm whether they are a threat. The same goes for when you are driving. If you feel like you are being followed, stop the car and let the other vehicle pass you.

Become a Hard Target

You need to look confident at all times so as to look less vulnerable to others. The more confident and aware of your surroundings that you seem, the less likely that you are going to be taken by surprise by an attacker.

Your Invisible Circles

We all have what we consider as our personal space, our boundaries. If we are around strangers, we have a set distance that we feel safe to stand from them. You can see this for yourself next time you enter an elevator, everybody moves to the corners. When somebody invades this personal space, there are a few things that you need to look out for.

Keep a watch out for their hands. Are they holding anything that could be used as a weapon or showing any intent of causing harm? Remember, even a rolled up newspaper or a magazine can become quite an effective weapon.

Look for bulges in their clothes that could be a sign of a hidden weapon.

Are they demonstrating verbal aggression or body language?

If you notice any of the above, you need to try to increase the distance between you and them. A 5 – 6 foot distance allows you enough time to react and assess the situation for any further action on your part.

Visualization

You need to learn to use visualization to assess a threatening situation and determine your actions. Visualize yourself in various threatening situations and think about how you would react, assess and protect yourself.

Intuition

Finally, you need to learn to trust your gut. We all have those moments when we have a feeling that something isn't quite right. Sometimes it is true and sometimes it is not but it is always better to be safe than sorry. If you learn to listen to your gut instinct, it can help to protect you.

Physical Fitness

You must remain fit as a prepper, If you need to run but cant make it to the end of the street, what good will that There might be times when you need to run, climb, move debris, swim and more. When be? When you first set out in getting fitter, do not be put off if you can only manage a single push-up or a single pull-up. It will be one more than you were doing before. Keep training and you will soon be adding more to that figure.

Walking, running and climbing are most probably going to be the activity that you do more than any other. The exercises that you need to be looking at to make this easier are:

Pull-Ups

Push-Ups

Dips

Box Jumps

Secondly, you need to improve your speed and strength which you can do using the following exercises:

Sand Bag Sprints

Ball Slams

Squats

Finally, we want to look at all those times you might need to crawl and pull things. You can do this with the following exercises:

Crawling with a Heavy Bag

Farmer's Carry

Bar Hangs

Kettlebell Swings

By trying to increase the amount of reps each time you perform the above exercises, you will be very surprised at how fast your fitness level can increase.

How to Sharpen Your Blades

If your blade is nicked you will need to use a coarse grit stone and start off by doing the following:

Hold the knife against the stone so that you will be grinding the edge as when the blade was new. The back of the blade should be about one blade width up from flat on the stone.

Gently stroke the blade across the stone evenly. Do not apply too much pressure and you can choose to go straight or in a circular motion. You should always cut in to the stone and never pull or drag your edge backwards. The edge of the blade should face the same direction as you stroke.

Be careful not to allow the edge of the blade to slide off the stone when you go from hilt to tip as this can cause a rounded tip to your blade.

Do the same number of strokes on each side of the blade.

If you just want to quickly touch up your blade, you will need a medium grit sharpener and repeat the above process. If you want a shaving edge, you will need a fine grit sharpener and again repeat the process.

How to Throw a Knife

It will take a lot of practice before you can throw your knives like a pro but stick with it and you wont regret it. When setting out, follow the tip below to throw your knives properly and effectively.

When holding the knife, you want to do so on the tip side between the thumb and the index finger. The tip of the blade should be pointed towards the palm of the hand.

Stand up with your feet shoulder width apart and one foot farther forward. (Much like a fighting stance). If you are right handed, put your left foot forward and vice-versa.

Look straight forward at the target and position both arms at the goal.

Move the throwing arm up and then back so that the knife is at the back of the head.

Quickly snap the knife forward as you move your arm down, swinging your weight from the back foot to the front.

Keep your wrist straight and your shoulder immobile at all times.

Keep practicing the above and you will be doing like the movies in no time.

Chapter 15: Tips, Tricks and Hacks

People have been practicing prepping and survival for years. That means there are a lot of people who have made some mistakes. Don't waste your time making the same mistakes. The following tips, tricks and hacks will help your prepping for survival go a little smoother.

- Use sturdy shelving made of wire or steel. Heavy wood is also an option, but it can collapse if too much weight is put on it.

- When assembling wire shelving, put the shelves on upside down. This will put the small lip facing upwards and help keep your food on the shelf instead of sliding forward.

- Use 5-gallon buckets with Mylar bags to store your dried beans, rice, flour and etc. Fill the bags and place them inside the bucket. The bucket will keep out rodents and protect from flooding, while the Mylar bag will keep the food protected from moisture and light.

- Place pasta and flour products in the freezer for a few days before adding to your food storage. This will kill the weevil eggs that are in all flour-based foods.

- Practice your fire starting skills in the rain or wind. Starting a fire in perfect weather is easy. Starting a fire with serious obstacles requires a lot more skill.

- Keep an extra pair of wool socks in your car at all times. If you have to walk for help and it is cold or raining outside, your feet need protection that only wool can provide.

- Wear a paracord bracelet. This is one way to always keep your cordage with you at all times. You won't have to worry you forgot it or it is in your other bag.

- Store tinder bundle material in your bug out bag and with emergency supplies. Tinder can be anything from shredded paper to dryer lint.

- Store your matches, lighter or even tinder in old prescription pill bottles. This is an excellent way to waterproof your gear.

- Pack garbage bags in your but out bag and make sure you have plenty on hand in your storage. Garbage bags can be used to carry water, wear as rain gear, used as a sleeping bag and plenty of other uses.

- Keep your food storage and emergency preps out of sight. You don't want to advertise what you have. Explain to the kids you really don't want them telling the kids at school that your crazy dad has a basement full of food.

- Store like foods together to help stay organized. You don't want your cans of fruits and veggies all intermingled so you don't know what you have of each.

These are some basic hacks. As you get going on your prepping journey, you will discover new ways to make your food storage a little better.

Chapter 16: A Prepper's Supply Checklist

A preppers checklist refers to a list of items you must have in your survival kit in the occurrence of an emergency. Now, I could go on about some 200 items you must have in supply, but for the sake of being brief, I will only discuss the most relevant and important.

- First on the list would be your food supply. You should have food stored at home, as well as a bug out bag with food supplies in case of evacuation.

- Water: Three days without water, and you are dead so, have sufficient water as well as a water filter.

- Portable shelter, more like a tent, or get some tools that would facilitate erecting a shelter.

- A portable energy source

- Flashlight or alternate source of light
- Fire-starters to light fire successfully
- Fuel for cooking/ powering your shelter
- Medical alcohol in your first aid kit
- Emergency medication including antihistamines, antacids, antibiotics, aspirin, and charcoal capsules in your first aid kit
- Toothbrushes, toothpaste, toilet paper, and other necessary hygiene-related supplies
- Shortwave radio, walkie-talkies, whistles and other communication devices, and spare batteries for these. One or a combination of these items is usually sufficient, depending on the nature of the emergency.
- Cash in hand

- Identification cards and medical records
- Firearms
- Kitchenware
- Any other item that you think is important in case of an emergency. Naturally, the type of emergency you are preparing for determines the supply checklist you would need to have.

Prepping: Getting Started

When disaster strikes, many of us hope that the government will be there to help. And it does. But one thing is true; even with all the budgetary allocation for disaster preparedness, when disaster strikes, the victims face it first hand and before any help can show up, you will probably have spent several hours, days or even weeks before help can come depending on where you are and the nature of the disaster. Well, unfortunately, that's how life is and in as much as we may want to say that the government might fail in its responsiveness, it may not be practically possible to help everyone when disaster strikes especially when the area affected is pretty large and is densely populated. And even if you were to go to your nearby rescue center, the truth is that they may be pretty ill prepared for an emergency thus making it almost impossible for them to manage the large group of those in need. Soon, you will start fighting for staples when the rescue center cannot keep up with the number. So what should you do at such times? Well, if you were not prepared, the best thing you can hang on is hope. But when you start prepping, you have control over what happens during a survival situation. You don't just wait for the government and aid agencies to rescue you. Instead, you take deliberate measures to ensure that you have everything you need to survive. But even with all the prepping, one thing is true; your mindset is your biggest asset when it comes to prepping. With the right mindset, you can do anything and overcome any challenge you may face. But whatever you do, it is important to keep in mind that:

- 3 minutes without air is enough to leave you unconscious

- 3 hours without synchronized body temperature is enough to leave you unconscious

- 3 days without water will leave you dead

- 3 weeks without food is enough to kill you

This means one thing; as you prepare for survival, you need to make sure that you prep in order i.e. shelter followed by water then finally food. With proper planning, assessment, and re-evaluation, you should be able to avoid/minimize panic and negative mindset and with that, your chances of survival will be drastically increased. So how do you prep? Where do you start? Well, it starts with preparing a survival pantry. Let's learn how to do that in the next chapter.

Setting Up The Pantry

Without food and water, you are pretty much doomed no matter what else you may be having. As such, before you can do anything else, the first thing you need to do is to set up a survival pantry (you can keep this in a survival bag or in a fixed pantry in your house) where you will keep enough food to sustain you for a few days into the disaster. For this, you will need to consider the perceived impact and the period you think the disaster may last. Don't just stockpile stuff that you have never eaten. Instead, stock stuff that you eat daily to avoid instances of discovering that you cannot eat something after wasting all the space and energy to keep a certain food. Nonetheless, what you pack in your pantry (or survival bag) is truly up to you but as you do that, you need to consider a few pointers:

Macronutrients: You should aim to have all the essential macronutrients in your pantry to ensure that you have a balanced meal. This should ideally comprise 5-20% proteins for toddlers & babies, 10-35% proteins for adults, and 10-30% proteins for kids and teens. As for carbs, you should aim for about 45-65% and for fats; you should aim to have 30-40% for babies & toddlers, 25-35% for kids & teens, and 20-35% for adults. As for the calories, you should aim for at least 1200 calories.

Tip about meals: Aim for about 500-700 calories per meal for each of the three meals then calculate that for the number of days that you want the food to last you. To help you stockpile fast, try to buy an extra item every time you go shopping. You will soon find yourself with a good quantity of such items. But don't just keep them forever; try to cycle such items in your everyday consumption to ensure you don't end up with expired food products. You can try to keep the new food at the back and those that have stayed for awhile at the front.

Tip: Keep in mind that there is something referred to as food fatigue caused by taking the same old food every other day. As such, don't just assume that any food is food during a survival situation. Try to have variety if you truly want to have a smooth time. You can pack such things like:

45-60 ready to eat meals packed in vacuum pouch bags.

Salt and pepper to make food tasty

Seeds: these are easy to pack and are light to carry around. Of course, if you are to survive in the wild for longer, you will somehow need to figure out a way of growing your own foods and not just relying on fish and meats. You can pack squash, corn, tomatoes, cantaloupe, lettuce, early carrots, broccoli, watermelon, Swish chard, onions, red beets, pumpkins, potatoes (white), cabbage, spinach, various herbs, sweet potatoes etc.

Grains

These will be made up of energy giving food and they include; pasta, rice, oats, cereals, pancake mixes, stuffing mixes and other similar foods.

Vegetables

These will serve as your major source of vitamins and minerals and they include a variety of canned vegetables.

Fruits

You can get additional fruit supply through foraging, but you need to pick your own fruits just in case. Items in this category will include all canned fruits and fruit juice that come in containers.

Protein

Basic food in this category include; canned salmon, canned tuna, peanut butter, canned lentils, canned legumes, canned soups, eggs and dried legumes.

Diary Food

These are other sources of proteins that will be needed and they will include packed dry milk, cheese, and yoghurt, canned liquid milk, soy milk etc.

Other Items

These are other miscellaneous items you will need in your survival bag and they include wine especially non-alcoholic ones because you will need to stay alert at all times to survive during this period. Others you will need will include: condiments like sauce, olive oil, butter, vinegar, ketchup, salt, ginger, pepper, dried herbs, sugar, and honey.

Tips For Stocking Your Bag

☐ Stick To Canned Items

You should always stick to canned items unless you are sure that your stay is a very short one. Canned foods can last for months if not years before they expire. That is the best option for you, not fresh foods that will get spoiled in a matter of days.

☐ Dried Items

You should always choose dried food to fresh ones; the moisture in dried foods has been extracted making them to last longer than fresh food.

☐ Think Long Term

You have to think long term when packing your pantry bag because you never can tell how long you will stay out there before help comes your way. So you need to include as many items as you can carry to last for a long time.

☐ Always Check For Expiration Dates

If you're buying canned food, it is advised that you take time to check the expiration dates for every item before purchase. Try to go for items with longer expiration dates.

☐ Balanced Meal

When packing your survival bag, ensure that the food in the bag is able to make you a balanced meal without your secondary source of food. That is why from the list I made on how to pack a pantry bag, I ensured that all the classes of food were present in the list to some extent. You need well balanced meals to stay fit, and fortify your immune system.

Important Note:

Even as you pack various foods, ensure to carry cookware; you can use a backpacker's cooking set, which you can fasten to the outside of the bug out bag or on your belt. But as you do this, ensure to carry one fork, a table knife and a strong spoon. You should also think of having a thick iron skillet or a cooking pot if need be.

Keep in mind that fire is life when it comes to survival. It will keep you warm at night and will help you prepare various foods comfortably. As such, don't under pack when it comes to prepping for fire because without anything else, knowing how to light a fire can keep you alive since you can hunt, catch various insects and prepare various foods. As such, ensure to have such things like 3 steel flint fire starters, bic lighters, waterproof matches and a hand lens.

And even as you do all that, you will also need to set up a survival bag i.e. the bug out bag that you will be carrying around with you or even place one at different places like in your car, your office, your home and other areas just to ensure that you always have enough survival stuff to survive for several days if disaster strikes.

Your Emergency Survival Bag

Although disasters strike when least expected, you can go a long way to save your life when disaster strikes by having a survival kit prior to the occurrence of the event. A survival kit is a bag where you put basic items you will need for survival during an emergency until help comes your way (enough to sustain you for at least 3 days). That probably explains why most survival kits are light and easy to carry with you.

Water: Ensure to have at least 3 liters of water in your survival bag. This should be enough to sustain you for 3 days. Ensure to have water purification tablets, water storage bottle or bag, water filtration bottle for treating all kinds of water, and purification straw for treating free flowing water.

Clothes: get a strong pair of shoes, a cap, pants, towel, shirts, windcheater, and undergarments to survive with for at least 3 days. The clothes you keep will depend on the survival situation you are prepping for as well as the climate. Simply ensure to have the right clothes for the potential disaster.

Shelter: Ensure that you have a tent or a tarpaulin in your survival bag. Another thing you can have is a light sleeping bag or preferably bothy bag (for shelter) or a bedroll.

Food: Ensure to have enough food (mainly canned or dried). You can opt for survival rations, energy tablets and ration heaters (for heating frozen foods)

First aid items: Have enough supplies for dealing with all kinds of injuries. In a survival situation, all manner of injuries will be present. As such, don't just have the simple first aid kit; go for something more advanced. For instance, your first aid kit should contain a suction pump to pump out poisonous venom, splint, cotton wool, needle and thread, Hydrogen peroxide or liquid spirit and some tablets. Others you can have include SAM splint (for immobilizing limbs), first aid kit (for treating minor injuries), burns dressings (for soothing and protecting burns), haemostatic powder (for preventing excessive bleeding, wound closing plasters, insect protector (insect repellents and coverings and sun protection (cream and lotion).

Utensils and containers: you need a cooking pot for preparing meals, for doubling as cups and plates and probably storing/purifying water. Also, try getting

Fire making equipment: Ensure to have gasoline lighters (Opt for the windproof option) waterproof matchbox etc. You should also ensure to have candles in your bag. You will also need to pack tinder (to help you start fire in any condition) and a flint for creating sparks under any condition.

Tools: In essence, you need to have such items like a survival knife, scissors, nylon rope, folding stick, hook, cutter, flashlight, batteries etc. You will also need compass for finding your way around. You will also need a saw for cutting wood and plastics, an axe for splitting wood, a small towel for digging mud and debris, and a crowbar for opening jammed windows and doors.

For lighting: Ensure to have a backup torch i.e. a pen torch, light sticks i.e. one time use glow sticks, hand torch for signaling through lighting and a head torch for keeping your hands free.

For heating and cooking: Ensure to have mess tins for cooking and heating on campfire, aluminum foil for minimal cooking, fuel depending on the stove, hexi stove, which is a stove that runs on solid fuel and solid fuel kettle if you have enough space.

For doing repairs: You can use a fishing line, sewing needle with thread, steel or brass wire, cable ties for repairing and binding, steel/brass wire for repairing and snaring, duct tape for fixing anything, nylon utility cord or paracord; you should have at least an item made with Paracord, either a bracelet or belt because a Paracord is very essential for your survival.

For battery: ensure to have alkaline batteries (AA or AAA), lithium batteries for the cold weather, solar charger that can charge batteries or charge devices, emergency charger for mobile and other devices etc.

Signaling and navigation: You can have the following items: Bright red jacket for warmth and signaling, mirror for camping and signaling, whistle without pea design that will not freeze, beacon i.e. a waterproof flashlight for signaling, compass for finding your way around and a satellite device whether it is a tracker or a satellite phone.

Communication devices: You can use a satellite phone, walkie talkie and radio

Note: Ensure that your survival bag is waterproof. Also, as you put stuff in your survival bag, it is important to remember that different survival situations will sometimes call for you to keep different things in your survival bag. For instance, the stuff you will keep when prepping for a flood or tsunami will definitely differ from what you will keep when prepping for a stay in a dessert. As such, you need to picture the scenario of what you will need in the particular situation that you are prepping for. You can add other items based on what you think you may need, but these are the basic items for survival you will need in case of emergency.

As you know very well, the stuff you will keep in your survival bag can only sustain you for so long. If you are to survive, you really need to ensure that you have all the information you need and probably practice how to live in the wild by scouting for water, food, making shelter and others. The rest of the book will focus on just that.

Making Provisions For Water

Water is one of the very important things you need to survive during an emergency. In fact I will keep water on top of my list because you can survive without other things like food for a longer period of time, but you cannot go without water for long. It may not come as a surprise to you that you can stay for 3 weeks which is approximately 21 days without food and still survive, but you can't survive without water for 3 to 4 days. This is to show you how important water is to your survival. So the question now is; how do you scout for water, or how will you make provisions for water when you are stranded in a desert or in an island?

Some of the ways you can source for water during an emergency include:

☐ Rain Water

If you are stranded in a desert, then this option may not be for you as it is very unlikely for rain to fall in a desert place. You can skip to other options mentioned below. Rainwater comes in handy in an emergency situation, especially if you are stranded in a bush land. You can look around for a small container (your survival bag should have pots, bottles and other containers) to collect water when it is raining or you can use a large leaf. To collect water using a leaf roll the leaf to give it a cone shape, fold the side you are holding and use the upper side of the leaf to collect raindrops. You can only use the second method to collect water which you will drink immediately because you can't save water using a leaf.

☐ Look For Streams/Waterfalls

Another method you can use is to walk around your surroundings to search for a nearby stream or waterfall. A stream or waterfall will take care of your drinking and bathing needs and it is actually the best option but if there isn't any stream near you, you can still use other methods. Ensure that your trip to scout your surrounding is done during the daytime when you can see clearly to avoid running into danger. Also, if you can't swim, remember to only use the riverbed.

When going on such a trip, you have to find a way of keeping track of your surroundings to avoid getting lost again. You can make marks on tree trunks as you go, or you can pick heavy stones and drop as you go or even tie twine on shrubs as you go.

Telltale Signs That A River Is Nearby

- Sound Of Rushing Water

The first sign that there is a river or stream nearby is that you will hear a sound of rushing water. All you need to do is to stand still and listen for the sound in the background. It might not always be a sound of rushing water; it can be a trickling sound if the water isn't fast moving.

- Via The Presence Of Some Insects

Some insects usually stay near water bodies and seeing them around means that there is a pool of water nearby. The most popular of them all is mosquitoes. Look out for mosquitoes in your environment; it's a sign that there is water not far from where you are.

- Birds can also signal where water is

Follow the direction towards which birds fly in the evening and in the morning.

- Damp Soil

Is the soil around the area damp? If yes, then it means that there is a stream or river nearby.

- Cool Temperature

Is the area cool? If the place is generally cool than other parts of the bush land, then it may be a sign that there is a waterfall nearby.

Also, look out for tracks of wildlife and lush green vegetation since this is a sign of nearby water. A muddy area is also a sign that there is water. Simply dig a hole then strain the water using a cloth

☐ Look For A Dry River Bed

A dry river bed can provide water for you, as some riverbeds still bring out water if you dig a shallow hole on it. If you see a riverbed around you, you can bore a hole with a strong stick (or use the hand shovel in your bug out bag) to see if you can get water from there. A dry riverbed is very easy to notice, because the ground looks all cracked up, while the soil is kind of moist if you dig into the soil.

☐ Soil Still Water

This method can be used to collect early morning dew to serve as water for your use. To use the soil still water method, you need to find plastic sheet, some stones and a container to collect the water.

When you get the items, you need to dig a hole in the soil; the hole should be dug directly above trees with big branches.

When you are done making the hole, you then place the container inside the hole, and place leaves all around the container. After that, use the thin plastic sheet to cover the hole then place bigger pebbles or stones on the edges of the plastic sheet to hold it in place while you place a smaller pebble in the middle of the plastic sheet. This way, dew that fall on any part of the sheet rolls to the middle and drops into the container. You can use this method to source for clean drinking water daily depending on how big your container is, or you can do this in several areas to help you collect enough water.

Other sources include lakes, oceans etc. Ice is also a good source of water but before you use it for water, ensure to melt it first since drinking ice can cause dehydration.

Here are some other ideas on how to collect water:

Wrap a leafy green shrub or tree branch using a plastic bag in the morning then insert a rock inside the bag to create a point where the water will collect. When the plant transpires, it produces moisture, which you will collect at the low point. As you do this, ensure the vegetation is not poisonous.

If you are near a beach (don't drink ocean water, as it is too salty and will cause dehydration), simply dig a hole that's 3-5 feet deep behind a sand dune (about 100 feet away from the waterline) then place rocks at the very bottom to ensure the sand doesn't become too active. You can then place wood around the sides if that is possible in order to ensure the walls do not cave in. You may be able to collect up to 5 gallons of water in a few hours. If the water is too salty, try moving a little farther away from the waterline. You can try the same approach in lakes; not necessarily the ocean.

How To Purify Water

Are there really ways in which you can purify the water you've collected so far, or will you have to drink germ filled dirty water just because you are stranded? The good news is that there are simple methods you can use to purify your water to make it safe for drinking and they include:

☐ Filtration With Cloth

You can use a clean cloth or wash out a dirty cloth then place it on a container to filter your water to remove debris and dirt before use.

☐ Boil The Water

This method is quite safer than the method mentioned above because it kills germs and other impurities. The best way is to boil the water first; ensure that you bring it to boil, bring down the water to cool down, and then filter with a clean piece of cloth. Ensure to aim for 10 minutes of consistent boil.

☐ Water Purification Tablet

If you're lucky enough to have a purification tablet in your survival kit, it will make the whole process easier; all you need is to drop the required quantity inside your drinking water and allow it to purify the water.

Tip: If you had packed the water purification supplies that we discussed earlier, you shouldn't have no problem in purifying water. But if you are short of supplies, boiling will be your next best option.

After water, the next thing on our discussion is food. How can you scout for food when you are in the wild when all your supplies are depleted? We will learn how to do that in the next chapter.

Setting Up A Survival Shelter

After you're done making provisions for water and food, the next thing on your agenda should be setting up a shelter to protect yourself from harsh weather conditions and wild animals. Although the shelter you will be setting up will not be anything close to your home, since it is an emergency situation, a survival shelter will give you the needed protection.

Items Needed To Set Up A Survival Shelter

In order to set up your survival shelter, you need to have the following items in place:

- Bamboo sticks or any other strong stick
- A sharp knife
- Twines, vines or preferable Paracord

How To Set Up A Survival Shelter

There are many ways to set up a survival shelter, but for an emergency, you can use the procedure below to set up a temporary shelter.

☐ Find A Clear Ground

You need to find an open space or a ground space without stumps; you can actually clear the ground around you to make an open space.

☐ Gather Sticks

Besides setting up the survival shelter, you will need to gather sticks to also make a fireplace. You can use this time and work on both tasks. For your fire, you need smaller and very dry sticks, but for your survival shelter, you will need to get stronger and bigger sticks.

☐ Set Up The Sticks

You need to set up the sticks to make your shelter. If the weather is too cold or you are not sure of the type of wild animals in the area, you may need to lay some sticks on top of each other to lift your shelter off the ground a bit.

After that, place the other sticks on the ground in a slanting manner to enable the sticks on one roll to touch the ones on the opposite. Continue mounting more sticks until you get to the desired length for your shelter.

Place a long stick across the slanted sticks and use a twine or the Paracord to hold them together.

Spread your emergency blanket or plastic sheeting on top of the sticks to serve as the roof; remember to create your entrance. If for any reason you don't have an emergency blanket or plastic sheeting, you can collect leaves and place on the sticks and use another set of sticks to help prevent them from blowing off when the weather gets windy in the night.

After setting up your survival shelter, you will need to make a fire in front of the shelter to keep wild animals away while you sleep, and to provide warmth for you when the temperature drops further at night.

How To Make A Fire Without A Matches Or Lighter

If you don't have a match or a fire lighter, you can use these alternative ways to set up fire:

☐ Bow And Stone Fire

This process is very easy; with a little practice, you can get the process perfectly. It involves using a bow and stone to produce sparks of fire. First, you need to make your bow; get a light stick that is flexible enough to bend.

Untie your shoe string or Paracord and use it to arch the stick. Simply bend the stick on both sides facing down and use the rope to hold the sides in place.

Face a wood surface and use your knife to carve a small hole on the wood;

Place some pieces of wool or tinder nest cloth to the hole; close enough to light it with fire sparks.

Place a side of the bow inside the hole and then place a stone on the end facing use; and hold it in place with your left hand and use your right hand to quickly turn the bow from side to side.

It will produce small sparks of fire to ignite the tinder.

☐ Battery And Steel Wool Fire

You can produce sparks of fire using a battery and a steel-wool. For this method, you will need a battery of at least 9 volts. Set the terminal sides of the battery (the terminals are the two metal sides that are slightly raised on the edge of your battery).

Bring a steel wool and rub both together to produce sparks of fire. Ensure that you have wool or tinder nest near that will catch the sparks to produce fire.

☐ Flint And Steel Fire

For this method, you use a flint and a piece of steel. Rub them vigorously together to produce sparks of fire but before proceeding with this method, you need to keep a small bare thread cloth nearby to catch the sparks of fire. The flint can be a small coal tar stone, and if you don't have any steel, you can use the blade of your knife as a substitute for steel.

The next part will talk about how to protect yourself while in the wild.

Chapter 17: Bartering Items

In an economic collapse, an act of war or civil unrest, the dollar isn't going to mean much when there are no banks or stores. Any major event is going to throw us back a couple hundred years and it won't be money that buys you the things you want or need, it will be the power of trading or bartering. One way to look at it is those who take the time to prepare and stock up are going to become the wealthy class in a world that has turned upside down. Those who didn't prepare, but kept a nice supply of money in the bank are going to be left in need.

You need to prepare to restock your supplies in a post-apocalyptic world or buy things you have run out of or absolutely need. Your money won't mean much, but your supply of chocolate could just buy you everything you need.

The following list includes items you will want to stock up on. They don't have to be for your personal use, but with the intent of using the items to barter.

• Chocolate bars, syrup, powder—People crave chocolate and will be willing to do almost anything to get a taste.

• Coffee—Coffee addicts will want to have that cup of Joe in the morning like they used to. When sleep is tough to come by, the extra jolt of caffeine will be appreciated.

- Alcohol-Stress and chaos tends to make people long for a drink. Stock up on a variety of alcohol, but know that you don't need to spend the extra cash on the good stuff. People will just want the numbing feeling of whatever alcohol they can get.

- Sugar, honey, and artificial sweeteners can store for long periods of time and will be in high demand. It is fairly inexpensive, but can buy you a lot.

- Tobacco—nicotine habits don't evaporate when the world goes sideways. People will be scrambling for a little tobacco. You don't have to buy cigarettes. You can buy loose tobacco and some rolling papers as a more cost-effective way to stock up on this high demand bartering item.

- Spices, salt and pepper-It may sound silly, but a lot of those freeze-dried meals and dried beans can be rather bland. A little salt or garlic powder can turn a bland meal into something delicious.

• Medicine and first aid supplies—add extra to your own supply to use for bartering or give them away out of the kindness of your heart. Bartering will be the new tender, but so will owing somebody a favor.

• Personal hygiene products—Toilet paper is one of those things that is truly hard to live without. If you have the space, stock up on the stuff. People will be willing to do a lot for a roll of toilet paper, soap or feminine hygiene products.

• Seeds—just because you live in the city today, doesn't mean you won't be eventually bugging out and headed towards open land you can cultivate to grow a steady supply of food. Heirloom seeds are an easy, inexpensive bartering tool. Only buy heirloom seeds. Stock up to use them as trade.

While these items will take up some precious space in your home, they are just as important as your food and water. There is a very real possibility you will not have absolutely everything you need after the world goes sideways. You need to be able to get those things and bartering will be the way to do it.

Chapter 18: Tips for Staying Alive in Urban Chaos

You hear a lot about preppers planning and training to survive off the land in the aftermath of a disaster, but you hear very little about the urban chaos scenarios. There are plenty of people who live in heavily populated areas that want to join the prepping movement, but need a little guidance and instruction. Surviving in the wild and surviving in the city require different approaches.

The following tips will help you survive urban chaos.

*You need to blend in. Change your clothing if you are going to go out into the streets. Wear what the others are wearing. Change out of your expensive suit and tie and put on "regular" clothes. Jeans, t-shirts and average looking shoes will help you blend in. If people think you have more than them, they will come after you.

*Travel in the wee hours of the morning, like 3 to 5 am. This is the best chance for you to move around without being seen by others. Late night is an option, but there will be plenty of other night owls roaming around looking for items. Go out for water or more supplies when the rest of the city is sleeping. Wear dark colors that won't stand out.

*Know your route. Study your route in advance so you know the quickest way to reach your goal without detection. Look for alleys you can duck into or buildings you can hide in if somebody comes along. Have an alternate route planned out in case your path is blocked.

*Have a get home bag prepared and stored in your office or your car. This would basically be a bug out bag, but you would be using the supplies to get home. You don't need a lot, just a supply of water, a few energy bars, a weapon and a few other survival items.

*Have a good supply of garbage bags on hand. You will need these to get rid of the trash in your home. It is truly crucial to your survival to keep your home sanitary. Trash build up is an open invitation to mice and other creatures that could end up making you sick.

Chapter 19: Survival Knife

Weapon Info:

The knife is the most indispensable out of all the weapons that aid survival in the wild. Having a sharp and sturdy knife enables you to cut and shape wood for numerous purposes, including building a shelter, constructing other weapons, tools, and cooking utensils, as well as chopping firewood to size. If you have flint, a knife can be used to generate sparks to start a fire. Knives can also be used to skin and gut animals, to peel and chop vegetables, and to harvest plants and fruit, not to mention the importance the knife holds as a weapon for self-defense.

Aside from the above reasons, the survival knife is first on our list of homemade weapons because it can be used in the construction process for all of the other weapons mentioned in this e-book.

How to make it:

When choosing the material for your blade, consider a high quality steel that has already been forged. Typically, all manufactured knives are forged. This means that the blade is shaped by hammering while heat is applied. Rather than forging your own steel, it's much easier to use steel that has already been forged.

It's best to choose strong steel for your blade, since it will maintain its sharpness for longer. However, make sure that the steel isn't too hard as it will chip away more easily. Most manufactured blades are made of stainless steel, which won't rust, but it is softer than carbon steel. Many blades consist of stainless steel mixed with carbon steel and the element molybdenum, which increases flexibility. There are numerous ready-made blades available that just require you to make a handle (skip forward to the final section for instructions on how to do this).

If you're planning to fashion your own blade, often the best forged steel to use can be found in flat files (except older files that are 100% carbon steel and can rust easily) and the blades from reciprocating saws. Files are especially good for making knives with small blades (up to a width of about 3/4 inches). If you want to make a wider blade, you can use a farrier rasp, which is used to maintain horses' hooves and horse shoes. Rasps are made of hardened steel and will maintain their sharpness well. You can buy secondhand rasps in farm supply stores for a very good price. Once you've chosen your file or rasp, you'll need to decide on a blade design depending on the intended use of your knife. Gut hooks, notches and indentations, and other elaborate designs are more difficult to achieve than a simple curved blade. More often than not, varying blade designs are more a question of aesthetic adornment rather than practical application.

Once you've decided on your design, mark and cut it out on cardboard first and then trace it with a marker pen onto the file or rasp. When shaping the blade make sure that you include a tang – the tapered point at the handle end - that extends the full length of the handle. This will provide a point of attachment for your handle and will strengthen your knife against breakage. At this stage you can drill holes into the tang, through which you can fix the handle once the shaping and finishing of the blade is done. Typically, a tang has four holes; two near the hilt of the blade, one in the centre, and one at the butt.

Important Rules to Remember for Survival

When a SHTF situation occurs, life will change. It make be brought about slowly, like the onset of a pandemic spreading across the country or something almost instant, a solar flare, natural disaster or the like.

The polite rules of society will break down very quickly and it won't be long before they are no longer in effect. In a world where people will have to scramble to survive, it will become an every man for himself way of life.

I am sure that human nature will prevail for a while, with your friendly neighbour lending a hand and groups of people banding together for the good of all, and warding off the bad guys by the powers of numbers. But, without any prior prepping or survival skills that 'nice guy' attitude isn't going to last long and it's only a matter of a few short weeks without food or water that we see the animalistic 'every man for himself' side of humans begin to take over.

This is when being more of an observer and not a talker can make the difference in your survival. You don't want people to know that you have supplies. If they know that you have them, the odds are very high that they're going to attempt to take them from you.

And what happens in a stressful situation is that people panic. If you get a group of people that didn't plan and don't have supplies, they're going to do things that they normally might not do.

If others find out that you have supplies, it's highly likely that they'll spread the word. Complaining, and resentment will kick in among a group of people. Then the herd mentality will start up.

Before you realize what's happening, there will be a run on your supplies and there will be too many people for you to be able to defend what your family needs.

In times of panic, there will always be those who will resent you for being prepared. They will see nothing wrong with making sure that you give them what they need - even if they have to take it by force.

There will also be those will take it simply because they want it to add to their own supplies. Difficult times always create a looting mentality. People will take things, even if they don't need it simply because it's there and they can.

You might not be the type of person who goes around saying what you have - and that's very wise. But it's important that you make sure that your children don't talk about it, either.

Kids don't always understand the importance of discretion, and sometimes they like to brag or think it's neat - but in this case, you'll want to make sure that they understand they have to keep quiet.

Any other family member or friend who knows about your supply should also be taught the importance of keeping your supply amount and more importantly, the location, a secret. What some people do to prepare for a SHTF situation when it comes to their supplies is that they have several different locations where food, supplies and equipment is stashed just in case one of them is compromised.

It can be inconvenient and a bit of a nuisance to do this, but it will still be the same cost. You'll just have to expend energy to find another storage area and keep up with more than one supply list. But it's for your benefit, because this way, if you do get one location's supplies taken from you, your family would still be able to survive.

By doing this, you are doubling your chances of survival by still having a food stash and should the worse happen and you are compromised, at least you have a 'fall back' plan.

You never know when you may be faced with that kind of situation and you're going to need to defend yourself or your family from people who would think nothing of harming or killing. In a perfect scenario, there wouldn't be a SHTF situation.

But they happen, so you have to be prepared to defend what's yours. And in a SHTF situation, everything would work out for you to be able to defend yourself and your loved ones.

There is hard evidence of the various ways people react to a disaster situation. For some it's a matter of helping others and being there for their neighbours and friends. For other it becomes the complete opposite – they look at it as an opportunity for personal gains for free. These gains are normally materialistic and in the early stages of a SHTF situation a looting mentality will rank high amongst these low-life scum.

However, as the situation worsens their priorities will change as they realise that food and water are really what they need. If you present yourself as a soft target to them you are in trouble.

Imagine this scenario - you might be off hunting for food. You could be cutting firewood or a number of other things to do with your survival. But, what if someone finds your loved ones alone, without the ability to defend themselves that could easily turn into an ugly situation. The low-life scum will not be bothered about the fact that they are only children.

Which is why every single member of your family needs to know what to do if this were to happen,

Even a small child can be properly taught about the seriousness of that situation. You want your children to be able to defend themselves from harm whether that harm is in human or animal form.

Your family should be trained to keep alert and understand situation awareness, how to raise the alarm and warn others as well as personal defence before it becomes a necessity. Everyone should be taught a degree of self-defence depending on their ability, size etc. They should also be taught how to handle any of the weapons you have with you. *but only to a level they will understand – in fact all family member must understand that, sometimes it's far better to escape than be injured in a fight.

This is, quite rightly, a contentious issue as there are so many different situations and so many what ifs. As well as so many things that could also go wrong, and go wrong big time.

Self-preservation for every family member must be foremost in their training, and knowing when to back off is as important as raising the alarm and fighting back.

This is one of the most difficult situations that you'll face. When you have to defend those you love and you know that they're counting on you to keep them safe, it can raise your adrenaline level somewhat!

Some people react very well to a serious threat. Others freeze. Those who freeze usually do it because they're not sure what to do. They don't know how to react because they haven't planned for it and didn't plan on needing to react to a threat like the one that they're facing.

Being compromised is something that needs to be considered in your bug out plan

When a SHTF situation happens, your family could very well come under attack - even from the people that you know and currently trust. Bad situations will often rob people of their conscious and normal moral behaviours.

They'll do things they never imagined that they'd do. An attack on your family can be scary. You might be called on to use lethal force to defend yourself and them. Remember that if you can remain calm, it will help your family.

If they see that you're okay, they'll be calmer and you need them to keep their cool, too. Prepare before the event of an attack. Know right now what you're going to do and what each family member is going to do.

The first thing that you should do is to establish a family safety or code word. The code word should be clear and not associated with anything else. You want this word to be one that in the event you have to use it, your family knows that it's serious and they know that a potentially dangerous situation has suddenly arisen.

Some people have a code word for various other potentially dangerous situations and it can be used universally to simply mean you are in grave danger and it's real.

You don't want to choose a word that's associated with anything else because it can be confusing for younger kids. For example, if you were to yell, "Run!" then your children might not realize exactly what you're talking about.

You want to give your family plenty of time to escape a bad situation. So choose a word associated with your plan. It can be something like "Go Time" or "Survive!"

Don't choose words like fire unless your family knows to get out of the house or the area to a predetermined safe area. You also want to make sure that you choose two words. Words that cannot be confused with others. All emergency services use the word 'Roger That' to mean they understood the message. There are no other phrases that can get misunderstood making it universally accepted and everyone knows what has been said.

This will help make it clear and easily understood. Two words are sufficient, the more words in a phrase that you use, the greater the chance that someone won't understand what you're saying. Keep it short and simple.

When you yell out the code word, each one of your family members must know what he or she is supposed to do. If you have small children, they should know that they either need to find an older sibling or a parent.

Or, you can train them to get to a predestined area and wait so that they're not in the way. A situation in your home may mean that you choose a room within the house that's a room where they can go to be safe.

If that's what you choose to do, this room should not be easily accessed from the outside. If it has a door that leads to the outside, someone trying to get in could very well find that door and have access to your family.

You don't want your family in a room where someone could easily break in through a window, either. Families that use a designated room in the house, know that if the code word is called out, that they're to get to that room.

When everyone is in the room, the entrance way should blocked. But you should be aware that if someone is determined to get to you or your family, they might not stop trying until they do gain access.

For this reason, you need to make sure that you have a means of defence and a means of outside communication with you. This would be a very extreme case and 'being under attack' like this is highly unlikely. But remember, we are talking SHTF and you can't rely on the police coming in to fight off the attackers.

The whole emergency system could be overloaded and your main phone system down. You'll want to have a way to reach others by having a couple of different communication devices in the room. Remember that your goal is to stay alive and keep your family alive.

If attackers breach the door of the room where you are, you'll need to be prepared to stop them from getting any closer to you. Sometimes, it won't be safe to even stay in a designated room in your home.

This is why you should always have a plan B. Every member of your family should understand what to do if it's not safe. An adult can make the call simply by using a word that's associated with a location outside the home.

Make sure that everyone knows they go to the outdoor location and they don't leave. It can be tempting for a family member to want to run back to try and save material possessions, but remember - it's about safety and survival - not fighting for what's inside your home.

Running to a second location can be a better defence than staying when you're outnumbered. There's no doubt that every part of surviving is going to cost you. Some of the costs will be as simple as taking the time to create a plan.

Other parts of survival are knowing what to do and when. But a great deal of the survival is making sure that you can fund your plan. This is where having a strategy can help.

You can't build a castle overnight. It's just not possible. However, stone by stone, you will get that castle built. It's the same for making sure that you have all of the survival supplies that you need.

Don't look at the big picture once you create your list. You might not be able to spend the thousands of dollars that you need to set aside a storage of food. In fact, you don't have to.

Instead, what you do is every time you go to the grocery store, you make sure that you pick up a few extra goods. You buy a little more than you need. You take advantage of the buy one get one free deals.

You can use coupons. You can even barter for goods. Each time you get more than you need, you put it in your survivalist storage area. It might take you several months, but you can stockpile your survival needs this way. You will be amazed at how much stock you can build in a short time.

You start out by creating a list and you work on it until you get all of the items on that list. You can also spend extra money on your supply needs. Instead of spending the gift card you get on another material thing that will only clutter your house, you put it toward buying something on your list.

Once you get all of the supplies that you need, you will have to periodically check on them. Your storage area will have to be checked to make sure that the environment is still suitable for storage.

Ideally your store room is cool, dark and water tight – store with these three essential conditions in mind at all times. Foods decay and spoil a lot easier when the temperature is too high, when they are in sunlight and if there's moisture in the air. Control these and your food will last way past the use by date.

You'll also have to rotate the supplies. This isn't something that will happen right away unless you buy foods that have a shorter expiration date. You don't want to do that.

When you shop, you always want to pay attention to the expiration date. You'll also want to make sure that you group similar items together in a storage bin, such as pastas, that you write on the outside of the container what the food is, when it was first stored. Do this in indelible ink that cannot be smudged or rubbed off accidently.

Most importantly you'll want to clearly mark the expiration dates. When you store foods that need to remain in a cool, dark place, you can't keep opening the storage container just to check the date.

That defeats the purpose of storing it. As the expiration dates draw near, you can use them yourself as part of your monthly grocery needs. Because of buying in bulk, it might be difficult for you to use large quantities before the expiration if you're not careful with the planning.

You might not be able to use a 25 pound bag of flour in a month, but if you pay attention to the expiration date, you'll know when to pull that flour to use so that nothing goes to waste.

Survival preparation was once an idea that very few implemented and many ridiculed. Over time, the masses started seeing horrific images unfold on live TV where natural disasters and man-made attacks caused the loss of lives.

Now, it's an idea that's becoming more mainstream. But there are always those who are resigned to preparing a plan to steal, rather than survive.

Prepping isn't something you do at the last minute. It's also not something you do haphazardly. It requires a methodical process of stocking up and knowing what your family's needs are long before you're caught in the crosshairs of a disaster that could spell the end for many individuals.

Hone Your Survival Skills

One of the best ways to prepare your family is practice. Your children's school regularly practices fire drills and perhaps tornado or other natural disaster drills, depending on your location. There is no reason not to do these at home. Educate your family on what to do in the event of a fire, tornado, etc. Do a practice run on a regular basis.

You can also practice blackout drills. Turn off the lights and electronics for a weekend. This is the best way to identify pitfalls in your preps and potential hazards in your home.

One of the biggest advantages of regular drills is it will help to mentally prepare you and your family. Panic comes from the unknown. If you plan and practice you will know what to do and when to do it. This will eliminate a lot of potential chaos and wasted time.

The Prepping Big List

The following list includes both basic necessities and some items that may be considered more "comforts" than "required."

Food and Cooking Supplies

• Multi – Purpose Survival Shovel

• Matches in waterproof container

• Charcoal (20 lbs. per person) and a charcoal lighter (store charcoal and lighter in waterproof container)

• Camp stove and fuel, grill or fire pit (you can make your own fire pit by digging a hole, lining with foil and cooking on an oven grate)

• Large pots and pans with lids

• Metal coffee pot

- Two pairs of channel-lock pliers
- Oven mitts
- Can Opener
- Aluminum foil
- Heavy-duty 30-gallon plastic garbage bags and twist ties
- Ziploc bags
- Paper towels and/or napkins, paper plates, plastic utensils
- Canned food, a minimum three cans of food per person per day (At least 3 days, preferably 15)
- Multi-vitamins and dietary supplements
- Coffee, tea, cocoa, powdered milk, powdered juice mix, etc
- Ball-point pen, labels, notepad, and tape

Sanitation

- Soap - an antibacterial liquid surgical scrub like Betadine is recommended. It would also be a good idea to have a supply of waterless hand santitizer and wipes in case water is extremely scarce after the quake. (Example: Purell and Wet Ones)

- Buckets with lids for human waste
- Detached toilet seat
- Heavy-duty plastic garbage bags and twist ties for disposing of waste
- Toilet paper (2 rolls per person per week)
- Clorox II powder (minimum 5–10 lbs.)
- Shovel or spade for digging latrine

Shelter

- 200 feet of 5 mil plastic sheeting and clothesline, rope and/or strong cord for a makeshift tent
- Shovel, pick, crowbar, axe, hammer, nails, saw, staple gun
- Crescent wrench for turning off gas supply

- Dripless candles and matches in waterproof container

- Flashlights, small AM-FM radio, extra bulbs, and batteries

- Extra shelter and sleeping gear (Example: ground cloths, tarps, tents, sleeping bags, inflatable mattresses or foam pads, tube tents)

First Aid

- First Aid Kit in a waterproof container or Ziploc bag

- First Aid Manual

- Buy extra small bandages, medical tape, anti-bacterial soap, alcohol, large dressings, bandage rolls, sling, splint, etc.

Survival Clothing

- Shoes with heavy soles or boots

- Work gloves

- Sweaters, overcoats, rain gear, caps, and gloves

- Spare eyeglasses or contact lenses

Conclusion

It is important that you practice preparedness, so you and your family can stay safe and sound, and fight all obstacles in case of strict SHTF situations. Use this guide to prepare in the best possible manner.

Thank you again for downloading this book!

I hope this book was able to help you to understand how to prep properly.

www.ingramcontent.com/pod-product-compliance
Lightning Source LLC
Chambersburg PA
CBHW071828080526
44589CB00012B/950